HOLY BIBLE

UNINVENTED

Why The Bible Could Not Be Made Up,
And The Evidence That Proves It

MIKE D'VIRGILIO

Copyright © 2022 MIKE D'VIRGILIO

Two Penny Publishing
850 E. Lime Street #266
Tarpon Springs, Florida 34688

TwoPennyPublishing.com
info@TwoPennyPublishing.com

All rights reserved. This book or parts thereof may not be reproduced in any form, stored in any retrieval system, or transmitted in any form by any means—electronic, mechanical, photocopy, recording, or otherwise—without prior written permission of the publisher, except as provided by United States of America copyright law.

All Scripture quotations, unless otherwise indicated, are taken from the Holy Bible, New International Version®, NIV®. Copyright ©1973, 1978, 1984, 2011 by Biblica, Inc.™ Used by permission of Zondervan. All rights reserved worldwide. www.zondervan.com The "NIV" and "New International Version" are trademarks registered in the United States Patent and Trademark Office by Biblica, Inc.™

For permission requests and ordering information, email:
info@TwoPennyPublishing.com

Library of Congress Control Number: 2022907928

Paperback: 978-1-950995-68-4
eBook also available

FIRST EDITION

For information about this author, to book an event appearance or media interview, please contact the author representative at: info@twopennypublishing.com

PRAISES FOR
UNINVENTED

The saying goes that in the 18th century the Bible died, in the 19th century God died, and in the 20th century mankind died. Whether true or not, one thing is certain: The historic Christian faith is grounded in an inspired, inerrant Word of God. Even though we are experiencing a renaissance in Christian philosophy and apologetics, too little focus has been directed towards making a solid case for the Bible. That is why D'Virgilio's book is so important and timely. As a bonus, his approach is unique and refreshing—nobody could make this stuff up! I highly recommend this important book and pray it gets a wide readership.

JP Moreland
Distinguished Professor of Philosophy, Talbot School of Theology, Biola University and author of *A Simple Guide to Experience Miracles*

By examining Old Testament histories from Abraham to David and New Testament reports about Jesus and Paul in cultural context, Mike D'Virgilio makes a robust and readable case against the view that these stories are invented fictions.

Peter S. Williams
Author of *Getting at Jesus: A Comprehensive Critique of Neo-Atheist Nonsense about the Jesus of History* (Wipf and Stock, 2019)

Have you ever wondered whether the Bible is what it claims to be? Could it be true that the Scriptures are simply made-up tales from an earlier, unenlightened time? My friend Mike D'Virgilio has wrestled with these questions, and you'll find his fascinating, faith-affirming answers in this fast-moving volume.

In plain language, Mike demonstrates over and over that the Bible wasn't somehow invented by credulous, simple-minded people, because there are too many marks of (as Mike puts it) "realness" in its pages. Whether you already believe, half-believe, or don't believe at all, Uninvented will open your eyes to the amazing reality of the Bible and what it means for your life.

Chris Castaldo, Ph.D.
Lead Pastor of New Covenant Church, Naperville, and author of *Talking with Catholics about the Gospel*

Uninvented is an accessible book for Christians looking to grow their faith and increase their understanding in the truthfulness of the Bible. Utilizing the criteria of embarrassment and dissimilarity, Mike D'Virgilio makes an approachable, cumulative argument that the Bible records historical details of real people, in real places, doing real things. This is what we Christians already believe to be true, but of which the skeptic is forced to contend.

Kurt Jaros, Ph.D.
Theologian at Veracity Hill, Executive Director of Defenders Media 501(c)(3), and Affiliate Faculty at Colorado Christian University

What I appreciate about Mike D'Virgilio's book is how he encourages readers to consider something many Christians haven't given much thought to before: could the stories in the Bible be made up? As Christians who already believe the Bible is what it claims to be, the arguments in Uninvented are a powerful reminder that the evidence in the text affirms that it is. Myths don't use imperfect individuals and imperfect lives to tell their story, but as we learn in Uninvented, God does!

Greg Brannon, MD

D'Virgilio holds court regarding the historical reliability of the Bible from a unique perspective, and given an honest jury pool of readers, wins the day. As he shows, the Bible as defendant does the real convincing as its own witness. I especially appreciate his approach: multiple angles and layers of evidence and commonsense inferences to the most likely explanations, calling out skeptics' often unwarranted naysaying. He critiques their beliefs as implausible or downright unbelievable. I would also add that his Socratic style of asking questions—and commenting on their weight—is engaging.

Though written for Christians, I think non-Christians will discover in Uninvented a fair, broad, and in-depth survey of multiple reasons to consider faith in the historic Person of Jesus Christ, what he taught, and his unique-in-history life before and beyond the grave.

Byron Barlowe
Probe Ministries International

To Greg Luther Smith,
from Mrs. Walker's 7th grade art class
to best friend forever,
and one of my biggest cheerleaders.

TABLE OF CONTENTS

Introduction 13

Chapter 1: The Bible and Its Critics 19
Liberal Christianity and Its Contradictions 19
The Enlightenment Sets the Stage 20
The Effect of the Enlightenment on the Interpretation of Scripture . 23
Biblical Criticism Gets Its Start:
    The Arbitrary Becomes the Authority 25
The First Liberal Christian 29
The Quest for the Historical Jesus 31

Chapter 2: The Christian Concept of Revelation 33
Creation and General Revelation 35
The Bible and Special Revelation 38

Chapter 3: The Inspiration and Authority of the Bible 43
The Idea of Biblical Inspiration 44
It's Either Verbal Plenary Inspiration or Nothing 48
Biblical Hermeneutics 51

Chapter 4: The People and History of Israel 55
A Creator God 55
Abraham, Sarah, and the Patriarchs 58
Moses and the Exodus 60
The Time of the Judges 62
King David 62
The Prophets 64

Chapter 5: Jesus—Too Popular to Make Up 67
You Don't Make Up a First Century Rock Star 67
The Jewish Diaspora.. 69
The Greek Language 71
Roman Roads 72
Memory... 74

Chapter 6: Jesus and the Jewish Nature of His World 77
John the Baptist and Jewish Messianic Expectations 78
John and the Reaction of Others to Jesus...................... 82
Jesus, a Friend of Tax Collectors and Sinners 85
Jesus and Women 87

Chapter 7: The Miracles of Jesus and The Apostles........ 91
The Nature of Biblical Miracles.............................. 93
Turning Water Into Wine 94
Miracles and Jesus' Authority 95
Jesus' Special Relationship to Water and Nature 98
Jesus Raises Lazarus from the Dead 101
Acts and the Apostles 102

Chapter 8: Jesus' Personality—
The Conundrum That Was Jesus 105
The Difficult and Unpredictable Jesus 105
The Un-Family-Friendly Jesus 106
Peter Turns into Satan!.................................... 107
The Transfiguration 108
A Samaritan Would Never Be a Jewish Hero.................. 110
How Not to Win Friends and Influence People 111
The Argument from Jesus.................................. 115

Chapter 9: Jesus' Teaching 117
It's All or Nothing at All: The Problem With Partial Jesus 118
The Forgiveness of Sin 120
The Hard Sayings of Jesus 121
Eat My Flesh and Drink My Blood 123
The Way, the Truth, and the Life 125
The First Will Be Last, and the Last Will Be First 127

Chapter 10: Jesus' Birth and Death 131
A Virgin Conception and Birth 132
Jesus, the Bastard Child 134
"Can Anything Good Come from Nazareth?" 136
Crucifixion and Death 136
Three Days in the Tomb 139

Chapter 11: The Resurrection 143
The Myth of the Dying and Rising God 144
What About That Empty Tomb? 145
How Did an Empty Tomb Turn into Christianity? 146
The Jews and Resurrection 147
Did They Steal the Body? 148
Other Options? 149
What Does the New Testament
   Actually Say About the Resurrection? 150
Why Are There No Depictions of the Resurrection? 150
The Criterion of Embarrassment 151
The Effect of the Resurrection 154

Chapter 12: The Apostle Paul 157
A Hebrew of Hebrews 161
Paul's Mission to the Gentiles 162
Paul's World Transforming Teaching 166

Concluding Thoughts	171
End Notes	177
Acknowledgements	185
About the Author	187

INTRODUCTION

The premise of this book is as simple as it is contested: The history and stories we read in the Bible are true and could not be invented; or in the vernacular, you just can't make this stuff up! We've also seen others shake their head in resignation say, "you just can't make it up." Before you is the unspoken truth: it's so hard to believe it's believable; it couldn't possibly be invented. I will argue that many stories in the Bible are unbelievably believable. Yet, we've been assured by our cultural betters, the intellectually "enlightened" since the so-called Enlightenment, that it *is* made up. The secular cultural messaging is that the Bible is make-believe. Unfortunately, many Christians are unaware that what we read in our Bibles would be highly unlikely to have been made up. The idea is not uncommon in apologetics literature, but I've found no book-length treatment of it. There are plenty of books, however, arguing that mere human invention is the *only* thing that can explain our Bibles.

In apologetics, there is something called the cumulative case argument. I found a good definition of this strategy at apologetics315.com:

> Arguments for the existence of God (or some other complex claim) that do not consist of a single decisive argument but rather try to show that God's existence makes more sense than any alternative hypothesis in light of all the available evidence.

As evidence piles up for a certain claim, it becomes increasingly probable the claim is true. As in a court of law, I like to think of this as beyond-a-reasonable-doubt true. My hope is, as we walk through the examples I present, and as they accumulate, you will come to the same conclusion I have, that the Bible could never have been invented.

I was prompted to write *Uninvented* because, as I read and wrote my way through the Bible over the last decade, I was continually amazed at the verisimilitude (the appearance of being true or real) I witnessed throughout its pages. We experience verisimilitude, or the lack thereof, whenever we read or see a work of fiction (or nonfiction). If executed well, we get lost in the seeming realness of what we're watching or reading. If not, we won't engage with it for long. So, as I was reading and writing my way through the vast scope of redemptive history, the seeming realness of it struck me with a force I do not remember experiencing before. The longer I read, meditated, and wrote, the more I came back to verisimilitude: "Wow, this reads real! As if this crazy stuff *actually* happened!" Like most Christians, I already believed all that crazy stuff *actually* happened, but this was different. Now, evidence *within* the text itself proved it to me. The more I made my way through the Bible, the phrase "there is no way this could be made up" kept popping up in my mind. The critics of Christianity, however, claim that it can be. This dialectic—made up, or not—is the heart of my argument.

Something that helped me formulate that argument is what I've come to call *the consideration of the alternative*. Tim Keller in *The Reason for God* points out something so obvious I wondered why I had never thought of it myself:

> But even as believers should learn to look for reasons behind their faith, skeptics must learn to look for a type of faith hidden within their reasoning. All doubts, however skeptical and cynical they may seem, are really a set of alternative beliefs. You cannot doubt Belief A except from a position of faith in Belief B.[1]

The more I made my way through the Bible, the more I realized the consideration of the alternative applied as much to the internal witness of Scripture, as to any other apologetic argument. The issue is never belief versus non-belief, but whether we believe in one thing or another. If we don't believe in proposition A, then we *must* believe in proposition non-A, whatever that alternative might be. The question is whether the truth claim of the alternative is more compelling, more plausible, and has more evidence to back it up. C.S. Lewis suggested people might want to doubt other things than just the Bible:

> Agnosticism is, in a sense, what I am preaching. I do not wish to reduce the skeptical element in your minds. I am only suggesting that it need not be reserved exclusively for the New Testament and the Creeds. Try doubting something else.[2]

We'll see how doubting the alternative plays out in the coming pages.

I previously believed you couldn't prove the truth of the Bible with the Bible. In one sense that might be true, but in another, it's nonsense. God's word is its own testimony; it reflects what it is, as the sun manifests what it is. I also wholeheartedly believe God's declaration in Isaiah (55) about the ultimate efficacy of His word:

> [10] As the rain and the snow
> come down from heaven,
> and do not return to it
> without watering the earth
> and making it bud and flourish,
> so that it yields seed for the sower and bread for the eater,
> [11] so is my word that goes out from my mouth:
> It will not return to me empty,
> but will accomplish what I desire
> and achieve the purpose for which I sent it.

As I thought through the skeptical claim that the Bible is primarily fiction, it led me to another thought related to the verisimilitude I experienced in the text. If the skeptics *were* right, then I would *have* to believe human beings not only made it up, but they were *capable* of doing so. Skeptics think it's the most natural thing in the world people not only *could* make it all up, but in fact, did—especially the supernatural stuff. As I continued to read more in apologetics, I consistently came across the assertion there is no way a certain biblical passage or story could have been invented. Reading the text, I now couldn't help seeing this everywhere, that what I was reading could *not* have been invented.

The consideration of the alternative helps us to see why. For example, if God is *not* Creator of the universe, then there *must* be another explanation for its existence. The only alternatives are materialism or pantheism; and neither is the least bit plausible, let alone provable. As I dove deeper into Scripture, I realized the same alternative thought process I had toward God as Creator or even His existence, applied to the Bible as well. There are two options as we come to the biblical text and its claims: It is either what it claims to be—God's inerrant, authoritative word, which tells us the truth about the ultimate nature of reality—or it is make-believe, merely human fiction to one degree or another. It is an inescapable either/or issue; and it cannot be anywhere in between, as we'll see. I've found it is far easier to believe Scripture is what it says it is—true history and God's revelation of Himself to His creatures. Just as in the title of a book I quote in these pages, *I Don't Have Enough Faith to Be an Atheist*, I also don't have enough faith to believe the Bible is make-believe. Many Christians who are not versed in apologetics don't know how much easier it is to believe the Bible is true than it is what the critics claim, fiction.

Obviously, it is essential that Christians can trust the Bible is true because our faith depends on it. I address this broadly in the first three chapters, which are critical to my argument. First, I deal with biblical criticism. Most lay-Christians are not aware of the successful and coordinated attack on the authority of the Bible rooted in the hubris of Enlightenment intellectual rationalism. Understanding the nature of that attack, and its weaknesses, is fundamental to realizing the compelling nature of what I discuss in the two chapters that follow: the idea of biblical revelation, and the inspiration and authority of the Bible. With that in place, we can see more easily how unlikely it is that all the stories in the history of redemption could be made up. I've concluded it to be impossible. I focus mostly on the gospels and the Book of Acts, but this idea applies to the entire Bible, and I spend a chapter scratching the surface of the story of God's redemptive work with the people of Israel. Being aware of the thoroughly Jewish nature of the biblical record is central to the argument of *Uninvented*.

As I implied above, part of the reason for Christian biblical insecurity is our secular cultural messaging, which is the result of hundreds of years of Enlightenment thinking, and the influence of biblical criticism. Over the years, I've come to believe apologetics is primarily a ministry to the church, to help strengthen the faith of Christians more than it is to convince non-Christians. For me, apologetics has been an indispensable theological discipline that immeasurably strengthened my trust in the truth of Christianity. So, this book is a labor of love for my brothers and sisters in Christ. If it happens to influence those who have not yet embraced Jesus as their Lord and Savior, all the better. My hope is, in these pages, fellow Christians will find in Scripture confidence they didn't know was possible.

CHAPTER ONE
THE BIBLE AND ITS CRITICS

LIBERAL CHRISTIANITY AND ITS CONTRADICTIONS

The Bible has endured an intellectual world war on its veracity for several hundred years. Most Christians aren't aware of this war—known as biblical criticism—nor how it has affected their confidence in the text of Scripture. What starts in academia never stays there, but eventually makes its way into the wider culture and becomes how we are programmed to see things. The average person thinks miracles can't really happen, and something written so long ago can't possibly be trusted as true history. Before anyone gets to the text, the assumption is skepticism; and Christians are not immune to these doubts. Because of biblical criticism, the default position of average Americans and Westerners is, "the hermeneutics of suspicion." In other words, the automatic approach to biblical interpretation (hermeneutics) for most people is skepticism. We need to challenge the hermeneutics of suspicion. I want to encourage Christians to focus on the text without the hundreds of years of skeptical noise in the background. To do that we must understand why there is such skepticism, and how it came about. Then we can expose that skepticism for the arbitrary unjust bias it is.

I don't want us, however, to throw the critical scholarship "baby out with the bathwater" because much good has come from biblical criticism. Critical scholarship has contributed to helping us better understand the meaning of biblical texts in their own historical context. The word *critic* can mean someone who is merely negative or critical; or it can mean someone such as a movie or literary critic, who is attempting to objectively assess the meaning or value of something. As the hermeneutics of suspicion implies, though, much critical scholarship appears to be assessing the text objectively but ends up being merely negative and critical. As we'll see, their assumptions demand it. Unfortunately, in the minds of many, the negative perception rules the day; and it's completely dominant in secular scholarly circles. Christians need to understand why we can confidently and with integrity reject the hermeneutics of suspicion.

THE ENLIGHTENMENT SETS THE STAGE

The anti-supernatural bias that informs this suspicion comes from the Enlightenment. From the perspective of its cheerleaders, prior to this time, people were stuck in the benighted (mostly religious) ignorance of the Middle Ages, or in some minds, the "Dark Ages." The movement in Western intellectual thought against the supposed Dark Ages arguably started with Francis Bacon (1561-1621), an English statesman, philosopher, and popularizer of the scientific method through empirical and inductive reasoning.[1] Modern philosophy, though, most agree started with a well-meaning pious French philosopher and mathematician, Renes Descartes (1596-1650). I say well-meaning because his goal was to develop a system of thought that would address the destructive effects of a growing skepticism of the possibility of true knowledge (partly because of Bacon). Unfortunately, his belief that absolute certainty was possible through reason alone, i.e., rationalism, inevitably led to skepticism, because without revelation, reason can get us only so far; and absolute certainty for finite beings like us is out of reach.

Having completely divorced his philosophical endeavors from his faith, the search for truth in Western thought took on the impetus to ignore religion, specifically Christianity, altogether. Descartes had two other motivations that led to the eventual rejection of God and the possibility of revelation among intellectuals. One was his insistence that reason had no need for any appeal to authority, primarily philosophical authority of past thinkers; and in due course, this would end up applying to the authority of Scripture and the Church as well. And the final nail in the coffin, so to speak, was his starting point for reason and thought. With God and revelation off the table, he could have only one starting point: the self. He was determined to start his pursuit of certain knowledge by doubting everything except what could not be doubted: his own thinking—in Latin, cogito ergo sum, or *I think, therefore I am.*

This was the ultimate Copernican intellectual revolution in the West. Instead of thought revolving around the reality of God and His revelation to man, thinkers increasingly ignored that (or like Descartes, walled it off in their private, religious lives), and sought truth exclusively through human reason. With the rise of science and knowledge, ironically given its inspiration by Christianity, intellectuals would soon question, and then completely reject, Christianity's ability to offer answers to the ultimate meaning of reality. We, they thought—mankind without God—could figure it out all on our own. For much of the 17th and 18th centuries, the Bible continued to have its spiritual influence on Western culture. Attacking it directly would have been too controversial. Nevertheless, the hubris and pretensions of Enlightenment intellectuals would eventually lead to their questioning everything about the Bible.

After Descartes, two of the most influential thinkers of the Enlightenment, Immanuel Kant (1724-1804), and G.W.F. Hegel (1770-1831), continued building on his assumptions. Together, their thinking profoundly influenced Western culture's eventual dismissal of God; but ironically both men, much like Descartes, thought they were Christians rescuing Christianity from the forces of intellectual skepticism. They also thought they were rescuing Christianity from the Bible and the Church. It isn't necessary to get into the details of their philosophies, which are terribly complicated; but we can say their philosophies were purely speculative and gave credibility to the idea that Christianity was possible without revelation. Both were trying to counter the thoroughgoing skepticism (can we really know anything?) of Scottish Philosopher David Hume (1711-1776), so a defense of the ability to acquire knowledge was necessary. Unfortunately, their ostensible cure only made the disease worse. Hume argued that miracles were "a violation of the laws of nature," but that, as logic tells us, begs the question (I'll explain this logical fallacy in chapter 7). As Enlightenment intellectuals in good standing, Kant and Hegel accepted Hume's naturalistic assumptions, and their thinking continued the assault on biblical supernaturalism.

It so happens that the man who arguably had the biggest influence on Western Enlightenment rationalism was not primarily a philosopher, but a physicist—Sir Isaac Newton (1642-1727)—a name familiar to every schoolchild, and himself a devout Christian. He had developed a system of physics that required an idea that in due course would become inimical to biblical faith: a closed material universe of cause and effect. Newton's universe came to be metaphorically compared to a machine-like mechanism, and the "natural" world would be increasingly seen and understood in purely mechanistic terms. Everything beyond nature was above it, outside of it, thus "super-natural." Eventually, the reigning assumption among Western intellectuals was that the natural world was the *real* world of everyday life, and anything outside of the material world wasn't real or didn't exist. Most of these intellectuals well into the 19th century accepted there was something outside of nature, but whatever he or it was could not impinge on *natural* laws.

Previously, I mentioned the arbitrary nature of skepticism. The claim that nothing outside of nature, including God, can break into and alter nature (i.e., the supernatural), is nothing if not arbitrary... completely, audaciously arbitrary. Benjamin Wiker tells us how the arbitrary became necessary:

> In the decades after [Newton's] death, the laws at first restricted, then ultimately denied, divine intervention. But

such was inherent in Newton's original formulation; for if every body can ultimately be reduced to Euclidean points in space, then nature is a closed system where the laws of motion not only describe completely every possible motion, but lock out any possible intervention.

Wiker further adds that Newton's definitions which allowed his physics to work, and thus required a "closed system," were never, nor could they ever be, empirically demonstrated; but they were asserted "by fiat," and the presupposition that allowed the system to work.[2]

The titans of the Enlightenment, and the biblical critics who came in their wake, accepted the anti-supernatural assumptions of their 18th and 19th-century intellectual environment and made the possibility of any kind of religious or metaphysical knowledge unattainable. Many would likely deny this, but anti-supernaturalism came to be accepted as a "fact" of existence; and anything otherwise came to be seen as an obvious myth, legend, or rank superstition. Religion, while perfectly respectable, for the time being, would be associated with "faith" and disassociated from the natural or material world.

THE EFFECT OF THE ENLIGHTENMENT ON THE INTERPRETATION OF SCRIPTURE

Given the centrality of the Bible to the Christian West, it could not be initially rejected outright by intellectuals and scholars. For most of them, that would have been inconceivable, but the Enlightenment brought significant changes about how the Bible needed to be interpreted; and these changes paved the way for the rejection of revelation, the rise of critical scholarship, and the flowering of liberal Christianity. It is important to identify the Enlightenment assumptions that drove the rise of critical biblical scholarship in the 18th and 19th centuries:

1. Reason is the standard and ultimate authority as to what the text means.

2. The universe is a closed system, so nothing supernatural can be allowed in. If there is a supernatural event in the Bible, it must in some way be explained naturally.
3. The Bible should be approached like any other book. We stand in judgment over the Bible, not the Bible over us. It is an historically conditioned human document, as fallible as any human, and full of errors. A divine author was ruled out before the text was ever assessed.[3]

These assumptions inevitably separated theology from history, so the two disciplines could have nothing to do with one another. Also, given the hubris of rationalists, Enlightenment assumptions led scholars to think an "objective" interpretation of the text was possible, which came to be called the "scientific" interpretation. They thought getting to the *true* meaning of the text apart from any presuppositions was attainable. To them, only religious people have presuppositions (which include the supernatural and are thus ruled invalid); and if we are to truly understand the text, we must rid ourselves of any kind of religious dogma. It then follows that the Bible is pretty much useless as an historical source. The biblical writers were all driven by ancient superstitions. It was therefore incumbent upon the critical (supposedly "objective") scholar to wade through all that non-history (the made-up stuff) to try to find the true history. This led to three standards that informed all critical scholarship:

1. Skepticism - You read the Bible as you would read any other ancient myth.
2. Analogy - You test historical accuracy by modern experience. If miracles don't happen now, they couldn't have happened then.
3. Coherence - Every event has a natural, historical cause, so it is invalid to bring in divine causes to explain historical events.

A good example of the mindset informed by these standards was Andrew Dickson White. An educator and historian who co-founded

Cornell University, he was instrumental in promoting the idea that science and theology have historically been in conflict, but not, he argued, with "true religion." Speaking of an 800-page tome he wrote on the subject, George Marsden writes,

> White proceeded to furnish a complete handbook for turn-of-the-century skepticism regarding traditional Christianity, his assault culminating in expositions of the incredibility of biblical accounts of miracles, the superiority of modern medicine and psychology over Biblicist supernatural explanations, and of how higher criticism had altogether demolished biblical credibility in scientific and historical matters.

All in the name of "saving pure religion," of course.[4]

Again, I describe this critical approach to the Bible as completely arbitrary because it's based on the anti-religious, anti-supernatural bias of the scholar. Why should we accept these assumptions? By what or whose authority should we accept the conclusions informed by them? These critical (pun intended) questions cannot be ignored.

BIBLICAL CRITICISM GETS ITS START: THE ARBITRARY BECOMES THE AUTHORITY

While biblical criticism became an industry and widely influential in the 19th century, it started with two thinkers: one who lived prior to the full flowering of the Enlightenment, and the other right in the middle of it. The first was Jewish Dutch philosopher Baruch Spinoza (1632-77), whose views were novel and controversial. For reasons related to his philosophy, he rejected that the Pentateuch (the first five books of the Bible) was written by Moses. Instead, he claimed they were written by many different authors from diverse backgrounds. He was so controversial that he was excommunicated from the Jewish community in which he lived. The other thinker who is given the official title of the father of biblical criticism is Hermann Samuel Reimarus (1694-

1768). Spinoza's ideas about the Bible percolated among intellectuals throughout the 18th century; but it wasn't until Reimarus, and then not until after his death, that the floodgates were opened for the phrase I used above, "the hermeneutics of suspicion." Attacking the Bible as a mere human document was too controversial prior to that, so his works went unpublished until he died. After that, the game was on. It became increasingly common, and acceptable, to question the text of Scripture in a way no other historical work would have been questioned. In the scholarly world, less than a century after his death, it would become the *only* acceptable way. N.T. Wright does a good job of distilling Reimarus' thought, and what would become the default perspective in the centuries to come:

> His aim seems to have been to destroy Christianity (as he knew it) at its root, by showing it rested on historical distortion or fantasy. Jesus was a Jewish reformer who became increasingly fanatical and politicized, and he failed. His cry of dereliction on the cross signaled the end of his expectation that his god would act to support him. The disciples fell back on a different model of Messiahship, announced that he had been 'raised,' and waited for their god to bring the end of the world. They too were disappointed; but instead of crying out in despair, they founded the early Catholic church, which to Reimarus may have looked like much the same thing. The thesis is devastatingly simple. History leads away from theology.[5]

The final point is crucial. Critics wanted to keep Christianity, but history, they claimed, couldn't support it; therefore they picked what they wanted, got rid of the supernatural, and through convoluted reasoning kept the religion. In due course, it enervated Christianity until there was nothing left but a shell; and eventually, radical secularism filled the vacuum.

Two other thinkers are worth mentioning. David Friedrich Strauss (1808-1874) was one of the most influential critics of the 19th century, and unlike Spinoza and Reimarus whose anti-biblical ideas were so controversial they were not released until they were dead, Strauss boldly and often proclaimed his rejection of supernaturalism. He claimed that in the gospels we find only the merest bare facts of Jesus' life, and that "the historical Jesus was buried underneath deep layers of myth, so much so that a biography of his life was nearly impossible to write."[6] This is a widely rejected position today, but it laid a solid foundation for the hermeneutics of suspicion that has become widely accepted by all non-Christian scholars. The other was Albert Schweitzer (1875-1965), a hugely influential genius whose work delegitimized the radical skepticism of Strauss and Reimarus; but he couldn't accept the traditional position that the Bible was the authoritative divine communication of God. He tried to walk a middle path which became a default position of many scholars, especially those who wanted to keep some form of Christianity but couldn't accept the supernatural.

The problem with much biblical criticism is highlighted by N.T. Wright in his 2018 Gifford Lectures (available on YouTube). Critics like Strauss and Schweitzer, about whom he goes into great detail, ignored the history and ideas of the first-century Jewish world. They did mostly criticism and a little history. They, and those influenced by them, argued that the gospels got it wrong, and so they were necessary to get it right. The gospels, they insisted, could not be taken at face value, and they would enlighten us, so to speak. Most of what they and their followers contend in interpreting Jesus and the gospels makes no sense at all in the first century, but a lot in the 19th and 20th. The German understanding of mythology and apocalyptic end of the world scenarios, in which they were immersed, had nothing to do with what first-century Jews actually thought.

It isn't necessary to get into details about the various schools of biblical criticism growing out of those who laid the foundation of the hermeneutics of suspicion. Once the Bible was rejected as the authoritative word of God, the result was a veritable Wild West of biblical interpretation. Whatever the various critical approaches, such as redaction, source, form, or literary criticism, what stands out about them is the arbitrary nature of these endeavors. The German higher critics,[7] a la Strauss and Schweitzer, were especially creative in their speculations. Dyson Hague, a conservative Canadian Anglican Evangelical, wrote of this German scholarly art form:

> [S]ome of the most powerful exponents of the modern Higher Critical theories have been Germans, and it is notorious to what length the German fancy can go in the direction of the subjective and of the conjectural. For hypothesis-weaving and speculation, the German theological professor is unsurpassed.[8]

If this was the case, and it was, we should inquire, "Why should we accept one scholar's guess over another?" Skeptics are fond of pointing out that among Christians there is a monumental amount of disagreement about many issues. True enough, but the disagreements are relatively slight when compared with what holds all orthodox Christians together, including the conviction that the Bible is historically accurate, and the authoritative, divinely inspired word of God. Without an agreed standard, why would anyone agree on anything? Leon Morris argues:

> [T]he view that what matters ultimately is what appeals to the individual's experience or reason is a profoundly pessimistic view. It means we have nothing from which to correct our errors, no way of knowing what is true or false once we have accepted an idea. If man's mind is the measure of things there is no way of getting back to the right way once that mind has gone off the wrong track.[9]

Instead of Scripture as their authority, Christians were now supposed to accept arbitrary assertions based on arbitrary assumptions of scholars who refuse to believe what the Bible declares about itself. Such an approach is less than compelling unless you accept their Enlightenment assumptions; then what choice do you have? You certainly don't have Christianity, but that's not exactly what happened. Instead of doing what they should have done when they declared the Bible was the product of mere human imagination—burned it and moved on—critical scholars tried to salvage whatever they could of Christianity; but it never looked much like Christianity, a la Kant and Hegel. What came out of all this was Christianity with a liberal bent.

THE FIRST LIBERAL CHRISTIAN

The first of these "liberal" Christians was Friedrich Schleiermacher (1768–1834), also known as the father of modern theology. He thought he could have it both ways, completely accepting Enlightenment assumptions, while keeping the Christianity of the Bible. When he was fifteen his father sent him to a Moravian (a brand of pietistic Christianity) boarding school where he began to doubt his faith, and his teachers couldn't or wouldn't help with his concerns. When he shared these doubts with his father, he was rebuked and threatened with hell. Needless to say, that is not the way to deal with a young person's faith struggles, but Schleiermacher found a way to keep his Christianity while at the same time accepting the intellectual assumptions of his age. Of these, 19th-century theologian Charles Hodge says:

> Schleiermacher... was addicted to a philosophy which precluded all interventions of the immediate efficiency of God in the world... Of course there is nothing supernatural in the Bible.[10]

Schleiermacher, however, didn't think this meant he couldn't keep Christianity. He just changed the locus of faith from God and his works objectively considered, to be something in the self. Hodge added:

> It is the fundamental principle of Schleiermacher's theory, that religion resides not in the intelligence, or the will or active powers, but in the sensibility. It is a form of feeling, a sense of absolute dependence… Revelation is not the communication of new truth to the understanding, but the providential influences by which the religious life is awakened in the soul… The Scriptures, as a rule of faith, have no authority. They are of value only as means of awakening in us the religious life experienced by the Apostles and thus enabling us to attain like intuitions of divine things. The source of our religious life is feelings.[11]

For Schleiermacher, and all the liberals who would follow, Christianity ceased to be primarily about God, but about us, our experiences, our obligations, our feelings. Its meaning moved from outside of us to inside. Why anything inside of us deserves to be authoritative is a mystery; yet after Schleiermacher as the template, liberal Christianity flourished. So much so that by the early 20th century all the major Protestant denominations became thoroughly liberal. This was true primarily in the seminaries and among church leadership. Most laypeople in the pews were unaware of what was happening and could scarcely understand the convoluted reasoning of critical scholars. Well into the middle of the 20th-century denominations and their churches kept a semblance of orthodox Christianity. While pastors and preachers used all the right Christian terminology, they meant something entirely different from what those words and concepts traditionally meant. The assault on orthodoxy had gotten so bad that by 1923 Princeton Seminary New Testament scholar, J. Gresham Machen, wrote a book called *Christianity & Liberalism*, in which he argued liberal Christianity wasn't Christianity at all, but a different religion altogether.[12] Without the supernatural power of God breaking into what appears the "natural" order of things, there is no Christianity. By the 1960s, these mainline Protestant denominations started losing people and cultural influence, and today are a shell of what they once were. A Christianity of human speculation isn't all that compelling or popular.

THE QUEST FOR THE HISTORICAL JESUS

I'll finish this brief survey of biblical criticism with a phrase that has been ubiquitous in the rise of liberal Christianity and tells you everything you need to know about its Enlightenment assumptions. The term was coined by Albert Schweitzer in a book titled *The Quest of the Historical Jesus*, published in 1906. The details of this quest aren't important for my argument, but the assumption is clear: The Jesus of the gospels wasn't historical, wasn't the real Jesus of history. What we see in the gospels is the "Jesus of faith," one that requires stuff we "know" can't happen, such as virgin births or people being raised from the dead, or the blind given sight, and the lame healed. As mentioned above, theology and history don't mix. The Jesus of faith is fine, you know if it floats your boat, but let's not confuse the Jesus of faith with the Jesus of history. And critical scholars (and the Enlightenment assumptions they don't think or admit they have) were ready to give us answers about who the *real* Jesus was.

Through various and sundry means, these scholars attempted to get through the fog of mythology to the Jesus of history. Reimarus, for example, portrayed Jesus as a less than successful political figure who assumed his destiny was to place God as the king of Israel. Schweitzer argued that Jesus was an apocalyptic preacher and that he and his followers believed in the literal and imminent end of the world. When Jesus didn't *really* come back from the dead, they concocted a story that he did. You won't be surprised to find that other scholars give us a Jesus as varied and arbitrary as the opinions of the scholars themselves. To them, Jesus was a mystery because the Bible gives us only a glimpse of the real Jesus. Once it was determined the miraculous Jesus didn't exist, there turned out to be as many "historical Jesuses" as the human imagination can invent! For example, Jesus was a failed prophet, or a great moral philosopher, or a cynic philosopher, or a violent revolutionary, and many others much more creative than these.

The irony is that whatever "historical Jesus" these scholars conjure up, he is not the Jesus of history at all. This critical approach, which is required if biblical revelation and authority are rejected and Enlightenment assumptions accepted, is entirely subjective. If we can't trust the biblical testimony of his closest followers, then anyone is free to define Jesus in any way they wish. Arbitrary is the best that can be done. I don't know about anyone else, but I have no desire to submit to the arbitrary authority of scholars who deny before they ever get to the text what the text insists it is. If we get beyond the fog of critical scholarship and the hermeneutics of suspicion, and let the text speak for itself in its historical context, we'll find a powerful and compelling case for the veracity of Christianity.

CHAPTER TWO
THE CHRISTIAN CONCEPT OF REVELATION

Christianity is a religion of revelation, not of human beings finding God—of us working to Him—but of God revealing and disclosing Himself to us, or else He could not be found. As sinful human beings, we do not seek God because He is our judge, jury, and executioner. In our natural sinful state, we hide when God shows up, as Adam and Eve did after the fall. Revelation itself tells us why, but human experience makes this perfectly clear; we can't live up to our own standards, let alone those of a holy God. That doesn't keep people from trying to find meaning in the conundrum that is existence, as we see in every permutation of religion throughout human history. By contrast, many Enlightenment thinkers wanted to rid the world of religion, so they insisted we could find meaning without revelation; human reason was all we needed. But Christianity counters that the *only* way we can understand the true nature of reality is revelation; we can't get that from man-made religion or reason alone. God must take the initiative to tell us the nature of things, or life is endless confusion. The history of philosophy is a testimony to such confusion—endless speculation and conjecture that contradicts and confuses, as do all world religions, save one. Life without revelation is like Winston Churchill said of the Soviet Union, "a riddle wrapped in a mystery inside an enigma." B.B. Warfield in *The Inspiration and Authority of the Bible* tells us why:

> The religion of the Bible announces itself, not as the product of men's search after God, if haply they may feel after Him and find Him, but as the creation in men of the gracious God, forming a people for Himself, that they may show forth His praise. In other words, the religion of the Bible presents itself as distinctively a revealed religion. Or rather, to speak more exactly, it announces itself as the revealed religion, as the only revealed religion; and sets itself as such over against all other religions, which are represented as all products, in a sense in which it is not, of the art and device of man.[1]

We must also understand the nature of biblical revelation. According to Herman Bavinck, revelation is God's self-revelation. "He is the origin, and He is also the content of His revelation."[2] This is an important point because, if we primarily see revelation as mere knowledge, God revealing certain things to us, we will miss what makes biblical revelation so, well… revelatory. God has primarily revealed Himself and continues to reveal *Himself*, His being and nature, in three ways: creation, Scripture, and Christ. We see all three in the first two verses of the book of Hebrews:

> In the past, God spoke to our ancestors through the prophets at many times and in various ways,[2] but in these last days he has spoken to us by his Son, whom he appointed heir of all things, and through whom also he made the universe.

God's ultimate revelation, that which defines everything else, is Christ. As we'll see, He spoke to us not only through the prophets, but also through the apostles, our New Testament. We also notice that revelation is spoken communication. God speaks, which shouldn't surprise us given we're made in His image; and we too speak. Revelation comes to us primarily in the words of God's redemptive acts in history. We learn this in the first sentences of the gospel of John:

> In the beginning was the Word, and the Word was with God, and the Word was God.[2] He was with God in the beginning.[3] Through him all things were made; without him nothing was made that has been made.

God's words speak through the Word that speaks through creation even as He speaks through the stories, propositions, and reasoning we find in Scripture. The Bible is a profoundly human book precisely because it is a profoundly divine one—not a book (or 66 books by 40 different authors) of mere human invention, despite what the critics claim.

CREATION AND GENERAL REVELATION

Uninvented is a book about the Bible, *special* revelation. The backdrop to the history of redemption we find in its pages is *general* revelation, or what God reveals of Himself to us in nature, His creation. I read through the Bible some years back and was impressed at how central the assertion of God as Creator is to biblical religion. The very first sentence of Scripture establishes that centrality:

> In the beginning God created the heavens and the earth.

So simple, so profound, so transformational in so many ways. As the Old Testament narrative progresses, we notice a drumbeat of contrast between God as Creator of all things and the worthless idols of the nations into which Israel was born. In an often comical way, the God of Israel, Yahweh, mocks the idols of wood and metal and stone because they are, uh, wood and metal and stone! Isaiah 44 is a wonderful example. Describing a man who is fashioning idols:

> [13] The carpenter stretches a line; he marks it out with a pencil. He shapes it with planes and marks it with a compass. He shapes it into the figure of a man, with the beauty of a man, to dwell in a house. [14] He cuts down cedars, or he chooses a cypress tree or an oak and lets it grow strong among the trees of the forest. He plants a cedar and the rain nourishes it. [15] Then it becomes fuel

for a man. He takes a part of it and warms himself; he kindles a fire and bakes bread. Also, he makes a god and worships it; he makes it an idol and falls down before it. [16] Half of it he burns in the fire. Over the half he eats meat; he roasts it and is satisfied. And, he warms himself and says, "Aha, I am warm, I have seen the fire!" [17] And the rest of it he makes into a god, his idol, and falls down to it and worships it. He prays to it and says, "Deliver me, for you are my god!"

As I said, comical, and sad. The idols of our age are not as crude and obvious, maybe not comical, but they are definitely sad. Both kinds of idols have no power; they can't *do* anything. Israel's God, however, created the universe; and so by contrast has *all* power. In Romans 1:20 Paul tells us:

> [S]ince the creation of the world God's invisible qualities—his eternal power and divine nature—have been clearly seen, being understood from what has been made, so they are without excuse.

The truth of these words has become increasingly clear as everyday science sees more deeply into the nature of God's created reality. From the unimaginable complexity of the cell to the astounding fine-tuning of the universe for life to the exquisite beauty and strangeness of nature, we are left dumbfounded before a being so powerful as its maker. God has left His almighty fingerprints everywhere. Whenever I doubt whether Christianity is true, I look outside and realize, if Christianity isn't true, then something else has to be. Atheism and pantheism can't explain what I see, or why I see, but Almighty God can! I like Calvin's words in this regard:

> [God] daily discloses himself in the whole workmanship of the universe. As a consequence, men cannot open their eyes without being compelled to see him. Indeed, his essence is incomprehensible; hence his divineness far

escapes all human perception. But upon his individual works, he has engraved unmistakable marks of his glory, so clear and so prominent that even unlettered and stupid folks cannot plead the excuse of ignorance.[3]

Creation, as God's most obvious revelation, is an especially important truth for Christians because secular cultural elites declare we are simply a product of chance via the Darwinian mechanism of random mutation and natural selection. Sure, Richard Dawkins admits, everything *looks* suspiciously as if it has been designed, but we know better, "wink, wink." The scientific "consensus" is that evolution is a "fact," and that random, unguided, "natural" processes are responsible for everything that exists exactly the way it exists. Read any book by an academic who is not a confessing Christian, and you'll see the amazing things "nature" and evolution can do. In fact, random, material processes really can't "do" anything. And it's not just that evolution is taught and promoted throughout the culture, but also everywhere assumed. Supposedly, we are just a product of random chance, merely lucky dirt. Mind you, very few people believe this, but it's almost impossible to escape the cultural consequences of the idea of Darwinian evolution.[4] That God is responsible for everything is just too obvious, but most people *live* as if we are random results of mindless material processes. We call them practical atheists; for most people, God isn't relevant to their everyday lives.

In a book written for Christians this is not a point I necessarily have to belabor; but Christians need to consistently remind themselves, their families, friends, and children, we are *not* a product of chance. Not too many years ago I realized how easy it was for me to be seduced by the lies of secularism, and that some things are "natural." For Christians, however, there is no distinction between natural and supernatural. C.S. Lewis points out that Mary's conception by the Holy Spirit was no more miraculous than any other woman's conception.[5] Sadly, I had never really considered that. Undoubtedly, he's right! Is not a new being's creation utterly miraculous? Are we really supposed to believe the process of creating a new life is solely "natural?" Nothing in all of creation is "natural" because all things are created and sustained by the word of God's power!

The goal is to get to a place where it is impossible to believe in naturalism/atheism (chance) as our creator, because that is impossible! If God is our Creator, *The* Creator, and if as the Apostle Paul says in Acts 17, He gives all life and breath and everything else, then we ought to act like it. The bottom line? General revelation ought to drive us to special revelation. We see through matter to the Maker of matter. It also ought to blow our minds, and cause us to worship, and consistently break out in doxology at such an incomprehensibly great and awesome being as our Creator God!

THE BIBLE AND SPECIAL REVELATION

The revelation of God in creation, however, can disclose only so much of His being. Without further revelation, the best we can do is guess what's behind all this awesome power and creativity; and as already stated, people have been guessing for all recorded history. Therefore, God has given us special revelation regarding His redemptive works in history, which is more awesome, powerful, and mind blowing than creation! One of the things I find most compelling is that the Bible exists at all. I marvel as I hold it in my hands every day, and what it took to get it there. Not to mention withstanding the attacks it has endured for the last several hundred years. It is miraculous in any understanding of the word.

The Bible is an unusual book because it isn't one book, but a collection of 66 different ancient documents written over 1,500 years on two continents primarily in two languages (Hebrew, Greek, and small portions written in Aramaic). It also had to be copied by hand once initially written, and then for another 1,500 years until Gutenberg invented his printing press in the 15th century. That's a lot of copying!

To modern people that means it must be riddled with errors and nothing close to the original text as it was written. Modern people would be wrong. I will not get into the details of textual transmission here because there are innumerable resources explaining why we can trust the text of our Bibles is, for the most part, the same text written by the original authors. But I will mention a fact that supports our confidence that it is.

Prior to the discovery of the Dead Sea Scrolls in the late 1940s, the oldest Hebrew manuscript of the book of Isaiah was from the 10th and 11th centuries (called Masoretic Texts after a group of Jewish scribes called Massoretes). A perfectly preserved text of Isaiah was found in one of the caves in Qumran where the scrolls were found, dating from 200 years before Christ. It so happens this text is identical to the text of Isaiah from over a thousand years later! Jewish and Christian scribes took their craft very seriously, so we can trust the Bible we read today is what the original authors wrote. This may not be a miracle in the technical meaning of the word, but to me it is miraculous, nonetheless.

What is even more amazing than accurate textual transmission over thousands of years is the Bible's coherence over 1,500 years of its being written. The outline of the entire book is contained in the first three chapters. The story unfolds from there on a beeline, albeit a slow one (God is never in a hurry), to its conclusion in the person and work of Christ. The more we learn about the Bible and its stories, the more difficult it is to believe it is a mere invention of human imagination. Instead, it appears to be divinely inspired. Critics and skeptics claim just the opposite, but we must ask ourselves how credible their claims are.

One way is to insist they defend those claims by the consideration of the alternative. Christianity makes absolute, exclusive claims to be the truth; and if those claims are not in fact true, something else must be. If the Bible is not what it claims to be, God's word, and it is not historically reliable as critics insist, then it must be made up. We should ask, could it be? Is it mostly fiction with a little history thrown in? For me, it takes far more faith to believe it was than to believe it is the historical, authoritative, inspired word of God. This applies to the individual parts or stories, as it does to the whole. As I mentioned in the last chapter, the default position toward the Bible is the hermeneutics of suspicion. Most people come to the Bible believing it can't be true, and thus are not able to let the text speak for itself in context. No other ancient work is approached from such an assumed skeptical position; but once Descartes did his thing in the 17th century, that became the "enlightened" way to treat the Bible.

Finally, the text of Scripture is more than just text, telling stories and teaching truth; it is the revelation of God himself in Christ. Thus, not mere words, but God's power *through* words, his divine Word (John 1:1). This power is inconceivably immense and beyond our comprehension, in a way, mere words cannot fully express because the words are part of the living Word (Heb. 4:12). Read the first chapter of Genesis to get a glimpse into this power. God created the heavens and earth—no small feat—and how did He do it? "God said." The phrase is used eleven times in the chapter; and when God said, it was. Our God never tries. We cannot comprehend a being so powerful that He merely speaks and something comes from nothing, and who continues to speak and everything comes from something! Such power is reserved for God alone, not creation alone. He's also deposited that same power in Scripture, our Bibles. When Jesus quoted Deuteronomy, that "Man shall not live by bread alone, but by every word that comes from the mouth of God," he was saying that God's word is an animating, life-giving force. The reading and studying of it, having it wash over and through and in us, is life itself! I love Moses' words to the people of Israel after God delivered the Ten Commandments (Deut. 6):

> [4] Hear, O Israel: The Lord our God, the Lord is one. [5] Love the Lord your God with all your heart and with all your soul and with all your strength. [6] These commandments that I give you today are to be on your hearts. [7] Impress them on your children. Talk about them when you sit at

home and when you walk along the road, when you lie down and when you get up. [8] Tie them as symbols on your hands and bind them on your foreheads. [9] Write them on the doorframes of your houses and on your gates.

How many of us treat God's commandments, His words entrusted to us in our Bibles, with such fanatical devotion? Might I suggest we ought to? If you're reading this book, it's likely I'm preaching to the choir; but we can never be encouraged enough to take Moses' words to heart. Something that might motivate us to strengthen our devotion is understanding that God's revelation through words goes well beyond words. Even though He uses words, reason, and logic, special revelation includes an inexpressible something that transforms beyond our ability to comprehend the text itself. We're meeting God himself in His word through the power of the Holy Spirit. This sounds kind of mystical, I know, but our finite minds can never completely capture the infinite. Paul hints at this when he addresses epistemology in I Corinthians 8. The context is food sacrificed to idols, and whether it's right to eat it or not. He says, "We all possess knowledge," and that "Knowledge puffs up, but love builds up." He adds, "Anyone who thinks he knows something does not yet know as he ought to know."

What is so wonderfully biblical about this is that it is not a call to skepticism, that we cannot know. Nor is it a justification for anti-intellectualism, that knowledge in and of itself is somehow corrupting. It is, rather, a call for epistemological humility. Our knowing is always limited, close to things as they are, but never absolute or exhaustive. We don't own the knowledge we possess as if it were ours. Knowledge then is safe only in the context of love, because it is used for God's glory and the benefit of others; it is revealed to us, not discovered by us. The words are bigger than us, than our minds can contain because they are God's words. As He says of His word through the prophet Isaiah (55), "It will not return to me empty, but will accomplish what I desire and achieve the purpose for which I sent it."

CHAPTER THREE
THE INSPIRATION AND AUTHORITY OF THE BIBLE

Now that we've established the idea of biblical revelation, we understand how general revelation in creation drives us to special revelation in Scripture. It will be helpful to understand *how* God conveys his word through the words of human beings, and *why* the Bible is our ultimate authority, given to us "by inspiration of God to be the rule of faith and life," as the Westminster Confession states. There are significant reasons to take the Bible seriously, including its historical reliability and textual transmission; but the most important reason is what the Bible has to say about itself. This is called the self-attestation, or internal witness, of Scripture. If the Bible is in fact the very words of God, as it claims, then it is the most important book in all the world; and we ought to treat it that way.

I like the way Loraine Boettner in his *Studies in Theology* puts this in the context of a discussion on the Trinity.

> [O]ur primary reason for believing the doctrine of the Trinity is... not because of any general tendency of human thinking to go in that direction, nor because of any analogies in nature, but only because it is a clearly revealed doctrine of the Bible. For those who accept the

> authority of the Scriptures, the evidence is conclusive. We do not here attempt to argue with those who deny that authority but refer them to the Christian doctrine of the Inspiration of Scriptures. Unless we agree the Scriptures are an authoritative revelation from God, it is useless to argue over the doctrine of the Trinity. The Christian finds the proofs for the trustworthiness of the Bible so convincing that he is compelled to accept its teaching concerning the Trinity even though his finite mind is not able to comprehend its full meaning.[1]

That is exactly right. As Moses is explaining in detail the covenant blessings and curses to the people of Israel in Deuteronomy 29, he puts these thoughts right in the middle of the explanation:

> [29] The secret things belong to the Lord our God, but the things revealed belong to us and to our children forever, that we may follow all the words of this law.

Once we accept the Bible as God's inspired revealed word, we can accept what it teaches, whether everything in it, like the Trinity, is fathomable to us or not. Given our finite, limited nature, that means there are a lot of "secret things" (not revealed); but what is revealed doesn't contain logical absurdities, even if there are many things we cannot fully comprehend. Do we insist we must fully understand something before we accept it as true in any other area of life, like biology, or photosynthesis, or electricity, or gravity? We do not, so why would we insist that of the Bible? We shouldn't.

THE IDEA OF BIBLICAL INSPIRATION

If you've ever talked to a non-Christian about the Bible, you've likely encountered a common objection: It was written by men a long time ago, so it can't be an inspired, divine document. Humans err, so the Bible errs. Good logic, bad assumption. It is logical if the Bible is *merely* a human document. We certainly don't deny it is a human document, but we contend it is a divine document as well, completely divine. How can it be both? The simple answer is God. If God exists and is an all-powerful, omniscient, omnipresent divine being, then for Him communicating His infallible will through fallible human beings is a piece of cake. It's not problematic in the least. It all depends on what someone assumes. Can we prove God exists or doesn't? No. What we assume depends on what we think of the evidence for His existence—if it is compelling or not. Even if someone is not completely compelled by the evidence, of which there is plenty, just positing a god as defined by what God is, biblical inspiration is perfectly reasonable. Let's examine what biblical inspiration means.

We might think because the word "inspiration" is used, God inspired the authors, got them jazzed up, so to speak, to write his divine material, so they wrote it; but, that is not biblical inspiration. The idea comes from the Apostle Paul's second letter to his young partner in ministry, Timothy (chapter 3):

> [14] But as for you, continue in what you have learned and have become convinced of, because you know those from whom you learned it, [15] and how from infancy you have known the Holy Scriptures, which are able to make you wise for salvation through faith in Christ Jesus. [16] All Scripture is God-breathed and is useful for teaching, rebuking, correcting, and training in righteousness, [17] so that the man of God may be thoroughly equipped for every good work.

The reason inspiration came to be the theological standard when communicating the divine nature of Scripture is that the King James Version translated the phrase in verse 16 as, "All scripture is given by inspiration of God." B.B. Warfield tells us why this is not the best translation:

> The Greek term has, however, nothing to say of *in*spiring or *in*spiration: it speaks only of a "spiring" or "spiration."

> What it says of Scripture is, not that it is "breathed into by God" or is the product of Divine "inbreathing" into its human authors, but that it is breathed out by God, "God breathed," the product of the creative breath of God. In a word, what is declared by this fundamental passage is simply that the Scriptures are a Divine product, without any indication of how God has operated in producing them. No term could have been chosen, however, which would have more emphatically asserted the Divine production of Scripture than that which is here employed.[2]

We'll look in a moment at what "Divine production" looks like, but Paul is referring to the Old Testament when he speaks of "the Holy Scripture," because it was some time before there would be a New. This tells us the primary reason we accept the divine authorship of the Old Testament: Jesus and the apostles accepted and taught it. The canon of the Old Testament, the books it included, was well established by the time of Jesus' birth, so we know which books "Scripture" refers to. The word Scripture itself (writing or graphé in Greek) is synonymous with "God speaks" and is used over 50 times in the New Testament. If Scripture said it, God said it; and its authority is never questioned. The same divine authoritative reference to the Old Testament is found all over the New Testament in three simple words, "It is written" (70 plus times). In addition to using this phrase throughout the gospels, Jesus further asserted the divine authority of the Old Testament in Matthew 5:17-18:

> [17] "Do not think that I have come to abolish the Law or the Prophets; I have not come to abolish them but to fulfill them. [18] For truly I tell you, until heaven and earth disappear, not the smallest letter, not the least stroke of a pen, will by any means disappear from the Law until everything is accomplished."

Jesus' reference to "the smallest letter" and "the least stroke of a pen" is famously translated in the King James as "jot and tittle." These marks have to do with the Hebrew alphabet, and how the very smallest parts of the letters are written. According to Jesus, there is something profoundly authoritative about the Jewish Scriptures; and he regarded every single bit of it from God. The law to which Jesus refers is generally a reference to the Pentateuch, the first five books of the Bible written by Moses; but the law is also used to refer to the entirety of God's written revelation to the people of Israel. In John 10, when defending himself against the charge of blasphemy by the Pharisees, Jesus quotes Psalm 82 and refers to it as "your Law." In the same passage he says, "and Scripture cannot be broken." We see all this come together in Luke 24 after Jesus has risen from the dead, when he tells the disciples on the road to Emmaus the entire Old Testament is about him:

> [27] And beginning with Moses and all the Prophets, he explained to them what was said in all the Scriptures concerning himself.

A little later he appears to his disciples, teaching them the same thing:

> [44] He said to them, "This is what I told you while I was still with you: Everything must be fulfilled that is written about me in the Law of Moses, the Prophets, and the Psalms."

By the nature of the case, the verbal divine inspiration of the New Testament does not have the overwhelming confirmation the Old does; but the case is not hard to make. We could explore this in a variety of ways in a more exhaustive study; but we know from one verse even during the lives of the apostles, their writings were seen as Scripture. Peter says of Paul (2 Peter 3):

> [16] He writes this way in all his letters, speaking in them about such matters. Some parts of his letters are hard to understand, which ignorant and unstable people distort, as they do the rest of the Scriptures, to their own destruction.

Peter and the Apostles knew their writings were divinely authoritative, and thus Scripture. Peter is illustrating what Paul says in Ephesians 2 when he writes, "God's household," the church, is "built on the foundation of the apostles and prophets." As the prophets proclaimed God's word, so did the apostles.

IT'S EITHER VERBAL PLENARY INSPIRATION OR NOTHING

This brings us to the concept of verbal plenary inspiration—or simply put, every single word, every jot, and tittle, is inspired, all of it breathed out by God. In the history of biblical criticism, some have argued the Bible *contains* God's word but is not *itself* God's word. Liberal Christians in the 19th and 20th centuries, and progressive Christians today, decide what to believe or reject based on current notions of cultural acceptability. The problem with this pick-and-choose approach is it can't escape being *completely* arbitrary. If the Bible's inspiration is not plenary, then why should *any* of it be true and authoritative? Good question. And who decides? Better question. If someone gets to judge what in the Bible is the real deal, why this bit over that, or that over this, how can their judgment be anything but completely arbitrary? Best question! Personally, I see no compelling reason why we should accept any human assessment of what in the Bible is and is not true. That would mean we would have to accept the authority of a certain person, or group of people, as to exactly what is true. Why should we do that? The most telling question. We shouldn't!

Inevitably, the liberal-progressive falls into the trap of 'having his cake and eating it, too.' (The proverb literally means, "You cannot simultaneously retain your cake and eat it." Once it's eaten, it's gone.) They want to accept the divine somewhere in there; but once they treat human insight as more authoritative than the text, the divine disappears, as it must. The Bible is either one or the other, divine or human. If it's human, then it's fallible and full of errors, since people are prone to error. If it's divine, however, then it's infallible and without error. Only then can we trust it fully as God's special revelation to us, His people. God used humans to write it, but every word in Scripture is there because He wanted it there. We might wonder how exactly God used humans without the human error bit sneaking in. The simple answer? He is God, and God by definition accomplishes things incomprehensible to His creatures. He does give us a glimpse through the Apostle Peter how this was accomplished, God speaking *His* word through human words (2 Peter 1:21):

> [21] For no prophecy was ever produced by the will of man, but men spoke from God as they were carried along by the Holy Spirit.

I've never understood those who have a hard time believing God could communicate through His creatures exactly what He wants to communicate, how and when He wants to communicate it. If He is the Almighty, omnipotent, omniscient, omnipresent God who created everything out of nothing by His own will and mind, then communicating to His creatures *through* His creatures is not a problem. The speaking, or writing, is of men *as* men, each unique in their own personality, family upbringing, education, culture, talents, circumstances; but it is simultaneously *from* God, of divine origin. The Holy Spirit made sure of it!

Jesus confirms this when he talks to his disciples before he accomplished our salvation on the cross (John 14):

> [25] "All this I have spoken while still with you. [26] But the Advocate, the Holy Spirit, whom the Father will send in my name, will teach you all things and will remind you of everything I have said to you."

The words *all* and *everything* are as comprehensive as it gets. We can trust all of it, because Scripture, though written by mere sinful men, isn't problematic if God is God, and he breathed out their words by his

Holy Spirit. John Murray, summing up the New Testament witness of inspiration, states:

> [W]e find that human authorship or instrumentality is fully recognized, and yet human agency is not conceived of as in any way impairing the divine origin, character, truth, and authority of Scripture. It is divine in its origin because it is the product of God's creative breath and because it was as borne by the Holy Spirit that men spoke from God. For these reasons it bears an oracular character that accords it an authority as real and divine as if we heard the voice of God speaking from heaven.[3]

We see in two of Peter's statements in Acts "the divine origin, character, truth, and authority of Scripture" written by a human author, in this case David. The first is in Acts 1:

> [15] In those days Peter stood up among the brothers (the company of persons was in all about 120) and said, [16]"Brothers, the Scripture had to be fulfilled, which the Holy Spirit spoke beforehand by the mouth of David concerning Judas, who became a guide to those who arrested Jesus."

And in Acts 4:

> [23] On their release, Peter and John went back to their own people and reported all that the chief priests and the elders had said to them. [24] When they heard this, they raised their voices together in prayer to God. "Sovereign Lord," they said, "you made the heavens and the earth and the sea, and everything in them. [25] You spoke by the Holy Spirit through the mouth of your servant, our father David:

> "'Why do the nations rage
> and the peoples plot in vain?
> ²⁶ The kings of the earth rise up
> and the rulers band together
> against the Lord
> and against his anointed one.'"

These verses confirm verbal plenary inspiration, and the Apostles believed it. The Holy Spirit breathed out the words David spoke, so David spoke the words of the Holy Spirit.

BIBLICAL HERMENEUTICS

I'll end this chapter with a brief introduction to hermeneutics, the scientific discipline of interpreting texts, biblical or otherwise. One of the main arguments of this book is that we need to be tethered to the text—either we accept all or none of it as divine. Once we are convinced we can trust the biblical text—that it is God's inspired revelation to us—there are rules for interpretation. When I was a young fundamentalist Christian, I thought it was just me and the Bible; God would enlighten me by his Holy Spirit, and I would understand it. My personal relationship with Jesus would be mediated through the Bible, without history, without theology, and with limited understanding of the context. To say my narrow focus invited interpretive problems would be an understatement; it was a recipe for misinterpretation. Christians will obviously never agree on every interpretation; but once we agree the Bible is the authoritative, inspired infallible word of the Living God, the disagreements are relatively minor.

So, as we come to the text of Scripture, we need to keep these four things in mind if we are to interpret rightly:

1. Authorial intent: what we can assess the author intended when he wrote the words.
2. Audience understanding: what the intended audience would have been expected to believe the words meant. This means

context counts, specifically the moment in history in which it was written.
3. Scripture interprets Scripture: never read a text in isolation from the rest of Scripture.
4. Scripture is all about Christ (Luke 24): the overarching theme of God's revelation to us is Jesus.

To fully benefit from the scope of redemptive history revealed to us in Scripture, we must understand how the puzzle pieces fit into the overall big picture. The pieces can only give us a limited picture, and an easily distorted one. Fortunately, we're not in this alone, which is why we *must* read more than just the Bible. We have easy access to books and the internet to help us grow in our understanding of the big picture, and all the little pictures that make it up. If we are to obey the imperative of Scripture itself to grow in our knowledge, then we will want to take advantage of the great minds who have come before us, as well as those of our contemporaries. The treasures are endless.

Finally, we learn in the Bible starting with Genesis 1, unless God himself opens our eyes, we are unable to see spiritual truth (Jesus' healing ministry was a real-life metaphor for this fact). Every Christian tradition would agree, although there is disagreement on the extent of spiritual blindness. All would agree, however, human reason alone can never unlock God's spiritual special redemptive revelation in the heart of sinners. So, I will end with a paragraph from the Westminster Confession that in 17th century English wonderfully captures the inestimable beauty of God's word, and the necessity of the Holy Spirit to enable us to understand it:

> We may be moved and induced by the testimony of the church to a high and reverent esteem of the Holy Scripture. And the heavenliness of the matter, the efficacy of the doctrine, the majesty of the style, the consent of all the parts, the scope of the whole (which is, to give all glory to God), the full discovery it makes of the only way of man's

salvation, the many other incomparable excellencies, and the entire perfection thereof, are arguments whereby it doth abundantly evidence itself to be the Word of God: yet notwithstanding, our full persuasion and assurance of the infallible truth and divine authority thereof, is from the inward work of the Holy Spirit bearing witness by and with the Word in our hearts (I:V).

CHAPTER FOUR
THE PEOPLE AND HISTORY OF ISRAEL

I start the meat of the book with the most unlikely people to have ever walked the face of earth—the people of Israel. The critics, however, have a difficult time explaining them away, not least anything that hints of the supernatural. Their story starts as supernatural as it gets.

A CREATOR GOD

"In the beginning God created the heavens and the earth." These famous words are the first words of our Bible. It is obvious to us today God, by definition, is the Creator of the universe, admitted even by those who don't believe in Him. He is the Creator! The only reason we believe this, though, is because of Judaism and Christianity; the former birthed the concept, and the latter brought it to the entire world. We have a hard time comprehending what a radical idea this was in the ancient world; we so frequently take it for granted, it almost seems "natural." It was anything but. The ancient world, no matter what culture or part of the world, knew nothing of an almighty, all-powerful Creator God until the Israelites came along. *The Gifts of the Jews: How a Tribe of Desert Nomads Change the Way Everyone Thinks and Feels* by Thomas Cahill, is a wonderful book exploring the many ways Jewish belief and practice was completely unique in the ancient world. Here are just a few of these gifts:

- **Fate:** Before the Hebrew people came along, life was viewed as something determined by inscrutable forces beyond any person's control. There was nothing to be done about it but submit. That changed forever when God revealed through Scripture that He created man, male and female He created them, in His own image.

- **Time:** Prior to the idea of "In the beginning God," all peoples of the world viewed time cyclically, one season moving into another, a wheel turning forever going nowhere. The people of Israel, by contrast, introduced the concept of past, present, and future; that history was going somewhere, something inconceivable to all other ancient peoples.

- **A transcendent, personal Creator God:** All other ancient peoples believed in gods who were visible (idols), and in fear of the forces of nature, believed they could manipulate the gods who presumably controlled the forces. The Hebrews introduced a concept no other peoples could conceive: a personal God, in some way like them, and the only true God. I can imagine an ancient person encountering these strange people saying, One God… who created everything? That's crazy! Cahill writes that the God of Abraham, "no longer your typical ancient divinity, no longer the archetypal gesturer—is a real personality who has intervened in real history, changing its course and robbing it of predictability."[1]

From what I can tell, Cahill seems to believe these "gifts" didn't necessarily come from a divine source. One can think, like Cahil, these "gifts" are indeed good for humanity, but still not accept they are a direct result of God's intervention in history.

At one point, writing about Abram deciding to listen to the call of God to leave his home and all he knew, Cahill states, "Out of mortal imagination comes a dream of something new…"[2] implying it was certainly *not* revelation from the God who called Abram. To me, that borders on the irrational. Here are a people who emerge out of the ancient world with ideas unlike any other peoples on earth. Where exactly *did* these ideas come from, so different and unique, if no other people conceived them, except the lonely old Hebrews? It's more plausible to conclude these ideas came from beyond human, mortal imaginations, that they were indeed revealed by God just as Scripture tells us. It's clear Cahill, from how he treats the text of the Old Testament, doesn't believe it is the divinely-inspired infallible word of God, and accepts the critical scholarly consensus that the Bible is merely a human book. Like the critics, Cahill has a naturalistic bias which keeps him from seeing the implications of the actual text. If no people on earth at the time could have conceived "In the beginning God…" then maybe it was in fact God!

In this chapter I'm able to present only a taste of the way I've come to read the Bible apologetically (as I read, it demonstrates its validity to me). My hope is that you take this perspective as you read the Bible yourself. Unlike skeptics and critics who start with a hermeneutics of suspicion, as we've discussed, we start with what we might call a "hermeneutics of trust," that revelation from Almighty God is not only possible, but actual. Leaving evidence of His fingerprints in creation, God has also left His fingerprints everywhere in Scripture. As we become more familiar with these fingerprints, we can put the burden of proof on the critics to justify their contention that a biblical story or event is made up. Normally, though, they assume their position without proof or evidence that the Bible is a merely human book and insist the burden of proof is on the Christian to prove it is not. We shouldn't let them get away with this. We must not let the assumption pass that something was or even *could* in fact be made up and turn the tables. This is upside down from the default skeptical position of the last several hundred years. Too many Christians accept that the burden of proof is solely on us, and then doubt creeps in. It does not have to be that way.

I won't reiterate all the details of the biblical stories, assuming you're somewhat familiar with them. If not, I suggest reading the stories I'm referring to so the references are clear and see if you come to the conclusions I do. You'll notice as you familiarize yourself with the narrative of God's people, He *never* makes things easy. In fact, He seems to go out of His way to make things particularly difficult, all the time, and in a myriad of ways that force them to trust Him, or not. It is striking how consistently this happens throughout the 1,500 years of the history recorded in the Bible. And not only this but the biblical characters are displayed as terribly human, warts and all prominently displayed. You would think a people writing stories about their history would make themselves look good, at least some of the time. Nope, not the people of Israel, eventually renamed Jews during their Babylonian exile (i.e., people from Judea). Christians, as we'll see, don't get off the hook either. It is difficult for me to comprehend a people, especially an ancient people, writing stories about themselves that consistently make them look bad. Knowing human nature, is that something we would predict if the biblical stories were merely fiction? And that were told over 1,500 years by 40 or so different authors? That I find hard to believe.

ABRAHAM, SARAH, AND THE PATRIARCHS

Take the stories of the Patriarchs, beginning with Abraham and Sarah, age 75 and 65 respectively, childless because Sarah is barren. God picks *this* couple to promise a child through whom all the nations of the earth will be blessed? Doesn't that seem rather strange? Sarah becomes frustrated after several years (after all, they're not getting any younger), and tells Abraham to sleep with her maidservant; and he does! This type of thing wasn't uncommon in the ancient world; but their actions scream, "God is a liar, and we don't trust Him to keep his word!" It is unlikely someone invents such a story about one of the founding heroes of their faith. The arrangement didn't turn out well. God ends up making them wait 20(!) more years before the promised child comes along. They name him Isaac, meaning "he laughs," because Abraham and Sarah found it amusing God would bless them with a child through their decrepit bodies. In the end God left no doubt—only *He* could make this happen.

One story about Isaac's life stands out as especially believable because it's so hard to believe. God tells Abraham to kill his son. What? Why in the world would God do that? You'll find the details of Abraham's supreme test in Genesis 22, and that God stayed Abraham's hand, so he *didn't* in fact kill his son, his only son Isaac. To me, this story appears so absurd it must be true. For those not fully convinced, it lends credence to the cumulative case of *Uninvented*. The point of the story, however, is not about an arbitrary God messing with His creatures to prove His power and control. Rather, it has specific redemptive-historical meaning that would point toward God Himself giving His only begotten Son, "because he will save his people from their sins." (Matt. 1:21) The Lord says to Abraham:

> "I swear by myself, declares the Lord, that because you have done this and have not withheld your son, your only son, [17] I will surely bless you and make your descendants as numerous as the stars in the sky and as the sand on the seashore. Your descendants will take possession of the cities of their enemies, [18] and through your offspring all nations on earth will be blessed, because you have obeyed me."

That offspring, or seed, is Christ, God's only Son whom He would not withhold for us either.

Isaac's son, Jacob who would later be renamed Israel, doesn't come off looking especially noble. Through him and his twelve sons, God would fulfill His prediction to Abraham (Gen. 15) that his descendants would be slaves in a foreign land for four *hundred* years. That's right, four hundred years. As I said in chapter 2, God is never in a hurry. God promises to bless Abraham with descendants like the stars in the sky, and the sand on the seashore; but there will be this little hiccup of four hundred years of slavery. Four hundred years prior to the time I'm writing this was 1622, which was about the time some Pilgrims sailed from England on the Mayflower and founded Plymouth Colony in present-day Massachusetts. That's a long time! While most people in the ancient world were slaves, it's odd that God would choose a people just to *make* them slaves. It's not the most flattering picture of one's ancestors, yet another thing I find difficult to believe unless it happened. In hindsight, we know captivity happened as a redemptive-historical picture of our slavery to sin. The next step in redemptive history is Moses and the Exodus, a picture of God's power as our only hope of rescue from that slavery.

MOSES AND THE EXODUS

God always chooses the most unlikely people, and Moses could certainly be voted the most unlikely to succeed. His fierce temper led him to kill an Egyptian who was mistreating a fellow Hebrew. So, at 40-years-old he had to flee Egypt for his life, settling in a place called Midian, where for 40 additional years he tended sheep and built another life. Then one day while he was tending sheep, Moses came across a bush that burned but did not burn up; and that is how God chose to introduce himself to Moses. What's amazing about this story in Exodus 3 and 4 is how pathetic it makes Moses look. As a hero of the Jewish faith, Moses stood second to none, and is revered by Jews to this day—but he was a coward! Every time God told him to do something, he made an excuse. He begged the Lord at one point to send someone else, "pretty please?" The text says that in response, "the Lord's anger burned against Moses..." Not a very flattering picture of the one who was to be the great deliverer of the Hebrews.

Exodus 4 is one of the strangest passages in the Bible and is surely the last thing that would *ever* be part of the historical record of the revered leader of a people, unless it was historical. God sent Moses to confront Pharaoh. On the trip to Egypt, we read these bewildering words seemingly out of the blue: "At a lodging place on the way the Lord met him and sought to put him to death. Then Zipporah took a flint and cut off her son's foreskin and touched Moses' feet with it." What? The Lord sends Moses to accomplish this great task, then on the way, Yahweh threatens to kill him? And his wife needs to come to the rescue? By circumcising their son, and rubbing the blood on Moses' feet? This passage is so bizarre it must be true! Even the not convinced would have to agree it is a very strange story to make up. The phrase, "You just can't make this stuff up!" could not be any more apropos. There is a back story for God's wrath toward Moses (Gen. 17), which makes him look even worse as a mediator and messenger of God's people. Being the author of the Pentateuch, Moses offers no explanation for his dereliction of duty, even though it almost cost him his life.

Much can be said about Israel's Exodus from Egypt. One thing is certain: God sure chose a very strange people to call his own. It really is stunning how pathetic they are in the portrayal of the Exodus, and their wandering in the wilderness for 40 years. They complained to Moses they had it better as slaves in Egypt, and that God brought them into the desert only to starve them. As I said, pathetic. Or take the story of the golden calf (Exodus 32), which is especially hard to fathom as fiction. Moses took a bit too long coming down from his mountain meeting with God, so the people convinced Aaron to make a golden calf to worship as their god who brought them up out of Egypt. This was only three months into their journey! Really? To top it off, Moses' partner and brother, Aaron, acted like a weakling and coward in the face of the people's rebellion. As we know, even Moses himself didn't make it into the promised land because of his lack of faith (Numbers 20:10-13, Deuteronomy 3:23-28). It is difficult to believe people would invent stories making themselves look so bad.

THE TIME OF THE JUDGES

The Israelites now enter the Promised Land of Canaan, and the narrative doesn't present as fiction either once they arrive. During this period of approximately 400 years (more of God taking his time), and prior to Israel's first king being crowned (Saul), the Israelites were ruled by judges. One would think those writing a history of their people might at least make some attempt at portraying them as noble or good, but not Israel. To say the book of Judges is not a flattering portrait of the people of Israel would be a significant understatement. The theme of the book is found in these passages reiterated several times: "In those days there was no king in Israel; everyone did what was right in his own eyes," and "The Israelites did evil in the eyes of the Lord." What is the point of telling readers this? Am I to believe the skeptics who claim with certainty little or any of this historical? Why record for all time your people are evil unless it was true, and that the history recorded in Judges had some larger purpose in redemptive history? The book ends with a story so shocking and horrific it's hard to believe it's in the Bible—an indication that the authors of the Old Testament wrote accurate chronicles of history.

KING DAVID

Until the late 20th century, many biblical critics denied there was an historical King David due to a lack of archeological evidence, but that changed with a significant discovery in 1993 (the Tel Dan inscription). If you've followed my argument thus far, you wouldn't need archeological confirmation of David's existence. Even though archeology is one of the Bible's best friends, the text itself provides plenty of evidence for the historical veracity of his life. When you read the story of David you can't help being driven to the conclusion this is a real man, living in real time, doing real things. Considering the Jews as a people again, and as great as he became, it defies logic that a king like David was mere fiction. (Read the details of his life in 1 and 2 Samuel, and I Chronicles). And remember, fiction did not exist in the ancient world.

The Lord eventually rejected Saul as king and commanded the prophet Samuel to visit Jesse in Bethlehem. God had chosen one of his sons to be king. The story, in I Samuel 16, is priceless. When Samuel arrived, he saw one of Jesse's sons, an impressive specimen; and He thought, "Surely, this is the Lord's anointed." Nope. Seven sons were paraded before Samuel, and none passed the test. Is this it? Samuel asked. Well, there is one more, the youngest tending sheep. Surely not him as the king of Israel? Yep, that's the one! What? A shepherd? As a King? That is counter intuitive, especially to an ancient Israelite; but God had been upending ancient cultural expectations for a long time, so why stop now! It was customary for the oldest son to be given the inheritance, and the power and authority that came with it; but God had a penchant for picking the younger or the youngest (e.g., Jacob and Joseph). So biblically speaking, the choice of David doesn't surprise us one bit; but culturally it was ridiculous, and very likely true.

The young David became a hero when he slew the Philistine giant, Goliath, and was eventually crowned king upon Saul's death. In due course he led the defeat of all Israel's enemies, conquered Jerusalem, naming it the City of David, and brought the ark of God to Jerusalem. The people of Israel experienced a peace and prosperity unlike any they had known—a land flowing with milk and honey as God promised Moses. Then we read one of the most famous stories in world history about David and Bathsheba, and we should wonder why it's there. The king seduced a beautiful young woman, and after committing adultery with her, had her husband killed when he thought he could no longer keep it secret. The great king, leader and hero of this ancient people was an adulterer and a murderer? Specifically, the one whom God picked because he was a man after His own heart? Ancient peoples were in the habit of making their leaders look good, not like this. As you look at the rest of David's messy life, it has a painful verisimilitude that lends credibility to the stories.

THE PROPHETS

I would love to get into the prophets, but space doesn't permit me to explore them in any detail. I will, though, comment on one of the greatest "can't be made up" stories in the entire Bible. I Kings 18 & 19 tells of the prophet Elijah's encounter with the prophets of Baal. If you're not familiar with the story, you must read it. It is so poignant in its pathos, so human in its depiction, and so real to life. The evil King Ahab and Queen Jezebel wanted Elijah dead (alas, a common experience for God's prophets) because he rebuked their apostasy and idolatry:

> [17] When [Ahab] saw Elijah, he said to him, "Is that you, you troubler of Israel?" [18] "I have not made trouble for Israel," Elijah replied. "But you and your father's family have. You have abandoned the Lord's commands and have followed the Baals."

Elijah was able to challenge the Israelites to witness a contest between the prophets of Baal and Yahweh saying, "How long will you waver between two opinions? If the Lord is God, follow him; but if Baal is God, follow him."

Elijah mocks the prophets, four hundred fifty of them to his one. Then with an awesome display of power, God proved he alone is God by sending fire down from heaven; and the people fell prostrate declaring over and over, "Yahweh is adonai (The Lord he is God)!" Checkmate! Elijah had all the false prophets killed, ultimately making the royal couple more determined to kill him. Terrified, Elijah fled for his life into the desert and begged for God to kill him! What? After what he just accomplished? God's chosen instruments always appeared to be under the gun, always in danger, always going against the grain, always fighting forces that are intent on destroying them. What a strange thing for a people to make up about their God, which compels me to believe they didn't; and it is the history it claims to portray.

This same is true for the rest of the story of the kings of Israel and Judah, including the people's idolatry and rebellion, and their eventual destruction and exile to Assyria and Babylon. It all reads real, especially in light of ancient human beings who everywhere else on earth tended to go out of their way to make their people look good. Unfortunately, critics and skeptics tend to ignore challenges like this that probably appear to them as trifles. It takes more faith for me to believe the critics' claims than it takes for me to believe the Bible is a reliable historical record. This doesn't even take into account how the events portrayed in the historical books of the Old Testament fit so perfectly into redemptive history—God's plan to save his people from their sin (Matt. 1:21). After his resurrection, Jesus points to the Old Testament declaring it's all about him (Luke 24). In that context, it's more intelligible as true history than as one big charade made up by some ancient religious zealots who had nothing better to do than lie about their people. The testimony of the New Testament is even more powerful in this regard.

CHAPTER FIVE
JESUS—TOO POPULAR TO MAKE UP

If I made my case that the Jewish people were unlikely to have been a mere human invention, the same holds for Jesus of Nazareth, the Jewish Messiah… times ten thousand. I'll reiterate my main contention because it's especially important to remember as we consider Jesus. Critics and skeptics insist the Bible and its stories are more or less fiction. Many would further insist that making up the biblical stories would have been a piece of cake. I contend they are wrong on both counts, especially the latter. Not only would it *not* be easy to make up the stories, but to the contrary I claim it would also not be possible. You'll have to see if my arguments warrant it, but I am convinced beyond any reasonable doubt it is true. Before I begin, however, as with our overview of the Old Testament, so with Jesus, I will assume readers have a general knowledge of the stories in the gospels to which I refer. If not, becoming familiar with them will help put my arguments in context, so I would encourage you to read them first.

YOU DON'T MAKE UP A FIRST CENTURY ROCK STAR

John Lennon famously (or infamously, depending on your perspective) at the height of Beatlemania in 1966 made an offhand comment to a journalist that the Beatles were bigger than Jesus. Well, we'll see in another 2,000 years; but the comparison of Jesus' fame to the Beatles is not an unapt comparison, at least for my purposes. In an age before ubiquitous distractions like ours, the daily humdrum and struggle for survival in the ancient world meant distractions were few and far between. When Jesus showed up, he would have been the talk around ancient water coolers all over the Roman empire—a "Beatlemania" of a different kind for the time. Jesus was as big as it gets in first century Palestine. He set the Jewish world abuzz, and because of his popularity the man we know as Jesus of Nazareth was certainly historical. As you read through the gospels you can see everything Jesus did was scrutinized and discussed by everyone he encountered, and word about him spread out into the Jewish population of the empire. The Jewish festivals that were celebrated three times a year in Jerusalem ensured news of Jesus, the possibly long-awaited Messiah (400 years), would spread far and wide.

Despite this, there are some who believe Jesus wasn't an actual historical figure, but a myth made up, as they say, out of whole cloth. About the gospels, the most reliable early records we have of Jesus' life, C.S. Lewis counters they don't read like myths:

> I have been reading poems, romances, vision-literature, legends, myths all my life. I know what they are like, I know not one of them is like this.[1]

The mythical Jesus claim is not taken seriously today by any reputable scholar, and it doesn't hold up under scrutiny. In fact, Jesus is one of the most well attested historical figures in all of antiquity, by far. Some critics rule out the Bible as historical evidence because the writers weren't unbiased, objective historians—as if such a thing existed in the ancient world, or any world for that matter. Yet, these critics would not doubt the historical credibility of Roman historians like Tacitus, Livy, or Caesar himself, nor Greeks like Herodotus, Thucydides, or Anaximenes, all of whom had points of view attempting to persuade their readers. No scholar today would reject the history because of the bias of the biblical writers, even as they discount the miraculous because of their anti-supernatural bias. The Bible has been corroborated by archeology so often they won't make the claim it's all a fairy tale, even though some atheists still insist it is.

Now that we have that out of the way, the reason news about Jesus spread so widely and quickly in the first century was because God had set the stage so adroitly by His sovereign, providential power. The Apostle Paul says in Galatians 4, "when the fullness of time had come, God sent forth his Son, born of woman, born under the law…" Three developments show us just how full the time had become:

1. The Jewish Diaspora.
2. The spread and acceptance of the Greek language throughout the Roman Empire.
3. The stability of Roman law and power, and the engineering that allowed them to build roads throughout the Empire, so travel was relatively safe and easy for the time.

THE JEWISH DIASPORA

Diaspora means a dispersion or scattering. After the reign of David's son, King Solomon (d. 931 BC), the nation of Israel began to slowly break apart into the northern ten tribes, Israel, and the southern two tribes, Judah. In 722 BC, the scattering began when the Assyrians conquered the northern kingdom, and the ten tribes were dispersed throughout the Middle East disappearing from the pages of history as a people. The two southern tribes had their dispersion from 597-586 BC when Babylonian King Nebuchadnezzar forced most of the people to go to Babylon, leaving behind a remnant of mostly the poor. The king allowed the Hebrews, now called Jews for the first time (those from Judea), to remain as a unified community and maintain their Jewish identity. Some of these Jews were able to make their way to other parts of the Middle East, while a third group made their way to Egypt and established Alexandria as an important center of Jewish learning. When the Persians conquered Babylon, King Cyrus in 538 BC allowed the Jews to go back to their homeland, but most stayed in Babylon (modern day Iraq). This is the period called Second Temple Judaism because the temple was rebuilt around 515 BC and stood until it was destroyed by Rome in 70 AD.

Because of the Diaspora, two important things happened that led directly to the spread of the gospel and early Christianity. One was the development of Synagogues. Jews who lived throughout what would become the Roman Empire developed Synagogues for a common meeting place to worship and for instruction. The Temple in Jerusalem could no longer be the center of their daily and weekly religious life because it was too far away, leading to a second development. Religious Jews throughout the Middle East, and even further, would make their way to Jerusalem for one or more of the three great yearly Jewish festivals—Passover, Pentecost, and Tabernacles (tents or booths). During Pentecost, Luke tells us in Acts 2, "there were staying in Jerusalem God-fearing Jews from every nation under heaven." The apostles began to speak in different languages because the Holy Spirit had come upon them, and these visitors' responses tell us just how far and wide the influence of Judaism in the Roman Empire had become:

> [7] Utterly amazed, they asked: "Aren't all these who are speaking Galileans? [8] Then how is it that each of us hears them in our native language? [9] Parthians, Medes and Elamites; residents of Mesopotamia, Judea and Cappadocia, Pontus and Asia, [10] Phrygia and Pamphylia, Egypt and the parts of Libya near Cyrene; visitors from Rome [11] (both Jews and converts to Judaism); Cretans and Arabs—we hear them declaring the wonders of God in our own tongues!"

Martin Goodman, in *Rome and Jerusalem* states, "The presence of the Temple turned Jerusalem into a magnet for Jews not just from the Judean countryside but from all over the Jewish world… International pilgrimage was encouraged by the ease and comparative safety of transport around the Mediterranean world ensured by Roman power."

He says further that the numbers of people in Jerusalem around the three festivals "exploded," and that the number of pilgrims was "staggeringly large."[2] Nineteenth century Jewish-Christian scholar Alfred Edersheim writes that "on the great feasts the population of Jerusalem and its neighborhoods… swelled to millions."[3] Whatever the actual number, it was a lot; and that meant for the three years of his ministry, Jesus' teaching and exploits were exposed either directly or indirectly to Jews and Gentiles all over the Roman Empire.

THE GREEK LANGUAGE

Alexander the Great was by any definition great. Born to the king of Macedonia (modern day northern Greece) in 356 BC, he studied for three years as a teenager under the also great Aristotle; and when his father was assassinated, he became king at the ripe old age of 20. As one of the great military generals of all time, he expanded the Greek empire all the way across the Middle East to India before his early death at 33. Most importantly, in God's providence, Alexander was passionate not only about conquering territory, but also bringing Greek culture and language to the territories he conquered (a process called Hellenization). Thus, 300 years later the Greek language was the "lingua franca" of what became the Roman Empire into which Jesus was born. By that time, Greek had become the primary language of most people in Israel, and the secondary language of the Jews who primarily spoke Aramaic, as did Jesus and his Galilean followers. This was the case throughout the Empire so that when the gospels and New Testament letters were written, the message therein was easily accessible and understandable to everyone. It was almost like God planned it that way!

We can also tie Alexander's influence to the implications the Jewish Diaspora would have on the eventual spread of Christianity. According to Edersheim:

> The immigration of Jews into Egypt commenced even before the Babylonish captivity… But the real exodus

commenced under Alexander the Great... There can be no doubt, in the providence of God, the location of so many Jews in Alexandria, and the mental influence which they acquired, were designed to have an important bearing on the later spread of the Gospel among the Greek-speaking and Grecian-thinking educated world.[4]

The hugely influential Greek translation of the Hebrew Old Testament called the Septuagint was translated in Alexandria between 300-200 BC. It was primarily this Greek Old Testament from which the New Testament writers took their quotations.

ROMAN ROADS

Finally, to put all the pieces together, Rome's power and rule of the Empire allowed them to build a transportation network of roads throughout the ancient Mediterranean world. Before modern transportation, getting anywhere of any distance was a slow and arduous process; but Roman ingenuity would alter that situation dramatically by ancient, and even more modern, standards. Primarily for military reasons, the Romans built 50,000 miles of roads. Do an internet search and you'll learn how these roads were notable for their straightness, solid foundations, cambered surfaces facilitating drainage, and concrete made to last from materials like volcanic ash and lime. And because of their ingenious design and careful construction, they remained technologically unequaled until as recently as the 19th century. In addition to the roads themselves, the Romans made sure they were well-protected and patrolled to ensure safe travel, including road signs and mile markers, state-run hotels, and way stations. Nothing like a rest-stop when you need it! There was also the influence of Roman power on the Mediterranean, as Tom Holland writes, "Never before had a single power controlled all the shipping lanes of the Mediterranean; never before had there been such a network of roads along its shores."[5]

We might be forgiven for concluding that God had something to do with this. After all, the unprecedented ease of travel the Roman road system made possible allowed the message of Christ's life and teaching, and news of his death and resurrection, to spread quickly. Craig Keener confirms that "the early churches throughout the Empire were already informally networked long before the writing of the gospels… urban Christians traveled, sent greetings to other churches, and so forth."[6] During his three years of ministry, we can glean from the gospels that Jesus visited Jerusalem for the feasts at least five times, and three times for the greatest of feasts, Passover. The swelling number of Jews and God-fearing Gentiles who visited Jerusalem and either encountered Jesus or heard the amazing tales of his miracles, would turn right around and bring back the telling of those tales to their friends and families throughout the Roman Empire. Critics would quickly retort this was a perfect recipe for the accounts of Jesus to get distorted, like the old telephone game. Maybe. However, it is not these accounts that make up the documents of Jesus' life we find in our New Testament; but that is a task many others have addressed and beyond the scope of this book. These three factors, then—the Diaspora, the spread and acceptance of the Greek language, and the Roman system of roads—allowed Jesus' life to become too well known to either invent or ignore.

We get a hint of how well known directly from Luke's gospel (chapter 24) when the resurrected Jesus meets the disciples on the road to Emmaus, and he asks them what they were talking about:

> [18] One of them, named Cleopas, asked him, "Are you the only one visiting Jerusalem who does not know the things that have happened there in these days?"

It is such things that everyone knows about, especially someone as memorable as Jesus, that are unlikely to be made up; nor are they so easy to distort beyond recognition.

MEMORY

My last contention is related to Jesus' "rock star" status. The last time I was reading and writing my way through the gospels, I was consistently reminded of an argument that Richard Bauckham makes in his book *Jesus and the Eyewitnesses*. It helped me develop my case, specifically regarding memory. Critics and skeptics often use the fallibility of human memory as the reason we cannot possibly trust the Bible's historical record. Most will grant there is some historical reality behind the biblical stories, but nothing like what we read in the finished product. I've already dealt with this from a critical and historical perspective in the first chapter; but I want to discuss why human memory is in fact an ally of biblical verisimilitude, or why it reads like real people, in real circumstances, doing and saying real things.

We all know from experience, as Bauckham admits, that "memory is fallible." On the other hand, there is something called "recollective memory" that is relevant to the memories of eyewitnesses, which is central to the argument Bauckham is making in his book: The gospels are eyewitness testimony that we can trust. He lists several factors about the power of this kind of memory which can help us trust the memories of those who encountered Jesus; but I'll focus on the first three, which illustrate how in certain cases memory is trustworthy:

1. Unique or unusual events.
2. Salient or consequential events.
3. Events in which a person is emotionally involved.[7]

We all have certain events in our lives that run like a movie in our heads no matter how many years have passed. Depending on our age, three huge world-shaking events evoke the response, "I'll never forget where I was when..." Pearl Harbor, the assassination of President Kennedy, and 9/11. My now 20-year-old son was in his mother's womb the morning of 9/11 when she ran into our bedroom hysterically exclaiming terrorists had flown airplanes into the World Trade Center.

I can see and feel everything about those moments as if they were yesterday. For my son, they are only images on a screen, but he can feel our incredulity that such a thing could happen when we tell him about it. It's the kind of stuff we remember vividly and do not forget. I would argue for first century Jews, Jesus was Pearl Harbor, the assassination of President Kennedy, and 9/11 all rolled up into one. We'll see why as we get into the following chapters.

We can all cite examples from our lives where the memories of unique, consequential events in which we are highly and emotionally involved are embedded into our consciousnesses. We can recollect those with an amazing amount of accuracy even if every detail isn't portrayed exactly as it happened. If we explore examples of such "I'll-never-forget-where-I-was" events in our lives and the lives of those we know, we'll realize we can come to the gospels and Acts with confidence that what we're reading actually happened. Keep "recollective memory" in mind as you consider Jesus portrayed in the gospels, especially in the Jewish context of the world in which he lived. Jesus was so radical and unusual, and the stakes so high, we might say he was completely unforgettable. To that Jewish context we turn next.

CHAPTER SIX
JESUS AND THE JEWISH NATURE OF HIS WORLD

Understanding the Jewish nature of Jesus and the world into which he was born, lived, and ministered is critical to the main contention of this book. It was the specifically Jewish milieu, for example, that made Jesus' popularity possible, as previously discussed. You might think it too obvious, hardly worth mentioning, to need to be told Jesus was a Jew; but for the first 150 years of critical biblical scholarship, this fact was mostly overlooked. Critical scholars generally admitted that some of what we read in the gospels was historical but argued the full-blown story we read in our Bibles was primarily a development of Greek and Pagan influences over a long period of time. Such a Jesus, however, entirely distorts the New Testament witness and has nothing to do with the Jesus who actually lived. Since the 1970s, biblical scholars have come to accept the thoroughly Jewish context of the gospels, which is the only way to really understand the Jesus of the New Testament. It would be much easier to make up a non-Jewish Jesus than a Jewish one. When coming to the gospels we must grasp this salient point: First century Jews could not conceive of a Messiah like Jesus, let alone invent one. In speaking of the Messiah's birth to come, Alfred Edersheim agrees:

> But of this whole narrative it may be said, that such inception of the Messianic appearance, such an announcement of it, and such manner of his coming,

could never have been invented by contemporary Judaism; indeed, ran directly counter to all its preconceptions.[1]

Being aware of the first century Jewish context of the New Testament is critical to knowing why the idea of *Uninvented* is so powerful, and why we can have confidence in the historicity of the gospel record.

JOHN THE BAPTIST AND JEWISH MESSIANIC EXPECTATIONS

The Jews had been waiting over 400 years for their Messiah—the one who would finally deliver them from the brutal repression of their Roman overlords, only the latest in a line of oppressors. Understanding Jewish Messianic expectations in the first century helps us to realize just how unexpected Jesus was. A good place to start is John the Baptist, and what led to his popularity at that point in Jewish history. The Old Testament ends with the Prophet Malachi, but the story seems to end without an ending. He begins the final chapter of his short book in the early 400s BC with these prophetic words:

> "I will send my messenger, who will prepare the way before me. Then suddenly the Lord you are seeking will come to his temple; the messenger of the covenant, whom you desire, will come," says the Lord Almighty.

This messenger was a preparation to remind God's people of his faithfulness; He will not forget them. In due course, Jews came to see this messenger as preparing the way for a Messiah. The word simply means anointed, and each king starting with Saul became the Lord's anointed, or the Messiah of Yahweh, who derived his reign from the heavenly King. So, the Messiah would be a king, in effect, the Lord himself because he would be representing the Lord. That the Messiah would *be* Yahweh himself, the divine Creator God of the universe, would *never* have crossed their minds—ever. Even non-Christian critical scholars find this difficult to explain. Monotheistic Jews do not invent a human who is also God, while to Greeks that would make some sense. Yet, read through the New Testament, and the writers clearly present Jesus as divine even if they can't explain or fully comprehend it. Jewish Messianic expectations of the time were primarily about rectifying the political disasters of Israel's history, once and for all. That would be a job for a divinely appointed human being, nothing more.

For a bit of the history leading up to the Baptist, after the Babylonian exile (586-538 BC), the Jews were ruled by the Persians until Alexander the Great defeated them in 333, who then conquered Judea shortly thereafter. When Alexander died, the Jews were ruled by a combination of Greco-Macedonian kings, until finally in 160s to 150s they gained some semblance of independence under the Maccabees. Less than 100 years later, however, the Romans gained control over Judea; and in 37, Herod the Great, a questionable Jew, was appointed "King of the Jews" by the Romans. There was a whole cross current of ideas among the Jews trying to deal with this centuries long upheaval, some through violence, some isolation, others religious observance. F.F. Bruce states:

> As the last pre-Christian century came to an end and the new era dawned, there were many in Israel who were looking for the kingdom of God, the consolation of Israel, the redemption of Jerusalem, to use the various phrases in which the nation's hope was expressed.[2]

Speaking of the heightened first century expectations, Alfred Edersheim writes:

> Within the land the feverish anxiety of those who watched the scene not unfrequently rose to delirium and frenzy. Only thus can we account for the appearance of so many false Messiahs and for the crowds which despite repeated disappointments, were ready to cherish the most likely anticipations.[3]

Even though the times were electric with anticipation, there was no consensus as to exactly what this Messiah would be. According to Martin Goodman:

> The fact that the picture of the Messiah which emerges from all the literature… is so confused, fragmentary and contradictory indicates that this confusion was standard among the Jews.[4]

Yet, most Jews at the time agreed on the broad outline of who the Messiah would be. According to one modern Jewish historian, he "was expected to be a king of David's lineage, victor over the Gentiles, savior and restorer of Israel."[5] The confusion and conviction about this Messiah made for a potential boiling cauldron when John came on the scene, and why he attracted such great excitement and crowds. The first chapter of Mark tells us how it all started:

> The beginning of the good news about Jesus the Messiah, the Son of God, [2] as it is written in Isaiah the prophet:
>
> "I will send my messenger ahead of you,
> who will prepare your way"—
> [3] "a voice of one calling in the wilderness,
> 'Prepare the way for the Lord,
> make straight paths for him.'"
>
> [4] And so John the Baptist appeared in the wilderness, preaching a baptism of repentance for the forgiveness of sins. [5] The whole Judean countryside and all the people of Jerusalem went out to him. Confessing their sins, they were baptized by him in the Jordan River. [6] John wore clothing made of camel's hair, with a leather belt around his waist, and he ate locusts and wild honey. [7] And this was his message: "After me comes the one more powerful than I, the straps of whose sandals I am not worthy to stoop down and untie. [8] I baptize you with water, but he will baptize you with the Holy Spirit."

Jesus and the Jewish Nature of His World

Having not heard a prophetic voice in so long, a man now appears who persuasively played the part of a prophet. John, however, was expecting the same Messiah as everyone else, one who would judge and rule an earthly kingdom. In Matthew 3, John warns of one who is coming in wrath and judgment, and he leaves no doubt about what the Messiah is coming to do:

> [12] His winnowing fork is in his hand, and he will clear his threshing floor, gathering his wheat into the barn and burning up the chaff with unquenchable fire."

From the beginning, though, Jesus doesn't seem to be playing his part. He starts messing with all these Jewish Messianic expectations, so much so that when things aren't working out like John thought they would, he doubts his own prophetic words.

After he was arrested, he must surely have thought, this was *not* how the kingdom of God would be ushered in by Israel's great and long-awaited Messiah. Having heard about the deeds Jesus was doing, he sends his disciples to ask him, "Are you the one who is to come, or should we expect someone else?" (Matt. 11). It would be very strange to make up a story about this long-awaited messenger being thrown into prison doubting everything he believed about the one he so recently and boldly proclaimed (Josephus, the Jewish Historian, confirms the basic outline of John's life and death that we read in the gospels). Jesus sends John's disciples back to tell John what they've seen and heard, the miracles he has performed, and references prophecies found in Isaiah. Yes, Jesus is saying, I am "the one who is to come." The problem, though, is that nobody expected the Messiah to be a divine miracle worker; and you can be sure as John was languishing in prison, he was expecting a whole lot more than a Messiah who healed a few people. It's unlikely that Matthew fabricates John's doubt if he's trying to convince people that Jesus was in fact Israel's long-awaited Messiah.

Lastly, it is odd that John, as the forerunner of the Messiah in the mold of Elijah, doesn't do any miracles himself, while Elijah most certainly did. I'll quote Alfred Edersheim again who nicely brings things together to make the point:

> The circumstance, that, according to the Gospels, no miracle was wrought by John, is not only evidential of the trustworthiness of their report of our Lord's miracles, but otherwise also deeply significant. It shows that there is no craving for the miraculous, as in the Apocryphal and legendary narratives, and it proves that the Gospel narratives were not cast in the mold of Jewish contemporary expectation, which would certainly have assigned another role to Elijah as the forerunner of the Messiah than, first, that of solitary testimony, then of forsakenness, and, lastly of cruel and unavenged murder at the hands of a Herodian. Truly, the history of Jesus is not that of the Messiah of Judaic conception![6]

Although we don't think so today because we're so familiar with the gospel stories, it is also odd that John baptized Jesus. Greg Keener makes the point:

> Given the embarrassment of some early Christian traditions (both in the canonical Gospels and in the early Gospel of the Nazoreans) that Jesus accepted baptism from one of lower spiritual status than himself, it is virtually inconceivable that early Christians made up the story of John baptizing Jesus.[7]

In the end, John the Baptist's life is a powerful testimony to the historical trustworthiness of the gospel accounts.

JOHN AND THE REACTION OF OTHERS TO JESUS

John's doubt highlights something strange about Jesus. Almost *everything* he says and does plays against type, against cultural and Messianic expectations. He befuddles and confuses, frustrates and intimidates, and elicits anger at times. These and similar emotions were even expressed by his followers and family. What he did not do is leave anyone indifferent. Since the novel or the idea of historical fiction didn't exist, it is difficult to imagine the gospel writers making up such a peculiar, often difficult, and enigmatic Jesus. Believing the gospels are the historical records of eyewitness accounts of Jesus of Nazareth is far more plausible. The reactions of Jesus' contemporaries must also be seen in their Jewish context to understand why the accounts are so credible. Even those who doubt the historical accuracy of the gospels and who deny the possibility of verbal plenary inspiration, can't help being fascinated and strangely attracted to Jesus. To this day, Jesus never seems to inspire indifference.

One of the great quandaries Jesus presented to his fellow Jews was the company he kept. First, Jesus was a Galilean; and if you're a first century Jew who wants to lend credibility to your message, you don't invent a Messiah from Galilee. It's the last place you would choose, unless it were true. In John 7, when Jesus is in Jerusalem for the Feast of Tabernacles, the people denied his legitimacy believing the Messiah couldn't come from Galilee (but from Bethlehem where Jesus was in fact born). When Nicodemus sticks up for him, other Pharisees reply, "Are you from Galilee too? Look into it, and you will find that a prophet does not come out of Galilee." When Philip tells Nathanael about Jesus, "We have found the one Moses wrote about in the Law, and about whom the prophets also wrote—Jesus of Nazareth, the son of Joseph," Nathanael responds, "Nazareth! Can anything good come from there?" Galileans were generally thought of by the more enlightened as boorish, uneducated, and religiously backward; and they sounded like hicks too. Think of it like urban, college-educated New Yorkers or Bostonians looking down on those hick-hayseed pickup-truck-driving southerners. But as everyone soon discovered, Jesus was no typical Galilean.

Not only was Jesus from Galilee, but he was born in humble circumstances, the son of a mere carpenter. Edersheim puts the implications this way:

> A Messiah, the offspring of a Virgin in Galilee betrothed to a humble workman—assuredly, such a picture of the fulfillment of Israel's hope could never have been conceived by contemporary Judaism. There was in such a Messiah absolutely nothing—past, present, or possible; intellectually, religiously, or even nationally—to attract, but all to repel. And so we can at the very outset of this history, understand the infinite contrast which it embodied—with all the difficulties to its reception, even to those who became his disciples, as at almost every step of its progress they were, with ever fresh surprise, recalled from all they had formerly thought, to that which was so entirely new and strange.[8]

This is a good summary of the unexpected Messiah Jesus turned out to be; new and strange indeed!

In Matthew 13 when Jesus comes back to his hometown after having built a substantial following with his teaching and miracles, his neighbors are incredulous: "Isn't this the carpenter's son?" They know his family, so they ask, "Where did this man get all these things?" And Matthew says, "They took offense at him." Certainly, the great Messiah can't live down the street, can he? Luke 4 portrays what could be the same event. Jesus is teaching in his hometown synagogue, and the people get so furious he's not talking like one of their homies that they drive him out of town and threaten to throw him off a cliff! Seriously? Why put this in such a story unless it actually happened. It's difficult to imagine inventing such a Messiah. Here's why this is a powerful apologetic: If Jesus said and did what was counter to every expectation and to the popular and accepted ideas of the time, who could have broken out of that paradigm, the accepted worldview, and invented Jesus? You would think if he was pretty much made up, he would at least do and say *some* things in line with the generally expected mores and traditions of the times; but he didn't. As we know, that eventually gets him killed.

Even his own family doesn't understand him. Early in his ministry we read these words from Mark 3:

> [20] Then he went home, and the crowd gathered again, so that they could not even eat. [21] And when his family heard it, they went out to seize him, for they were saying, "He is out of his mind."

And these were the people who knew him best! In John 7, Jesus' brothers are trying to talk him into going to the Feast of Tabernacles, but Jesus didn't want to go because the Jewish leaders were looking to kill him, and his time had not yet come. John tells us:

> [3] Jesus' brothers said to him, "Leave Galilee and go to Judea, so that your disciples there may see the works you do. [4] No one who wants to become a public figure acts in secret. Since you are doing these things, show yourself to the world." [5] For even his own brothers did not believe in him.

Doesn't this read real? Why invent a Messiah who can't even get those closest to him to believe and trust in him as the Messiah? Maybe his brothers really couldn't accept that their brother was in fact Israel's long-awaited Messiah; and like other Jews of the time, Jesus wasn't acting the way they thought the Messiah should act.

JESUS, A FRIEND OF TAX COLLECTORS AND SINNERS

Jesus also kept strange company for a supposedly Jewish Holy Man. From the beginning, Israel was a people set apart. It started with Abram being the only one Yahweh chose out of all the people in the ancient Near East to begin creating this peculiar people of God. The Jews seemed to have missed the bigger point, though, that it really wasn't all about them in the end. God promised Abram "all the people on earth will be blessed through you" (Gen. 12). God also spoke through Isaiah saying Israel would be "a light to the Gentiles" (Is. 42:6, 49:6). Yet, by Jesus' time, pious Jews wouldn't even eat with Gentiles! And when Jesus did, it was a scandal. We read in Matthew 9:

> [10] While Jesus was having dinner at Matthew's house, many tax collectors and sinners came and ate with him and his disciples. [11] When the Pharisees saw this, they asked his disciples, "Why does your teacher eat with tax collectors and sinners?"

Tax collectors, of whom Matthew was one, were considered traitors to their people, and human scum. Yet Jesus chose a tax collector to be one of his 12 closest followers. Luke 15 tells us:

> Now the tax collectors and sinners were all gathering around to hear Jesus. [2] But the Pharisees and the teachers of the law muttered, "This man welcomes sinners and eats with them."

If you want to make up a credible story about a Jewish holy man, a Messiah no less, this is not how you do it. In Luke 7 there are two stories that, to a first century Jew, would have been scandalous. For example, in one, a Pharisee invited Jesus to his house for dinner, and an uninvited woman "who lived a sinful life" showed up with an alabaster jar of perfume. It's a powerful scene, knowing who Jesus was, and shocking if he's just another Jewish holy man:

> [38] As she stood behind him at his feet weeping, she began to wet his feet with her tears. Then she wiped them with her hair, kissed them and poured perfume on them.
>
> [39] When the Pharisee who had invited him saw this, he said to himself, "If this man were a prophet, he would know who is touching him and what kind of woman she is—that she is a sinner."

Pharisaical Judaism was not known for its mercy and grace, to say the least. This woman's sordid reputation obviously preceded her, and Jesus was allowing her to touch him. In their eyes, this rendered Jesus in that moment religiously unclean. That a man claiming to be a rabbi and a holy man of Israel did this was disqualifying. Pious Jews would likely not include such a story if they wanted other pious Jews to believe them.

The other story is not about Jesus' cavorting with "sinners," but interacting with and helping a Roman Centurion. Such fraternizing with Israel's hated rulers bordered on treason. The story is told a bit differently in Matthew 8 and Luke 7, but the gist is the same: Jesus treated this Roman's request to heal his servant with respect and granted his wish. To add insult to Jewish injury, he even praises the man in a way that would infuriate Jews who loathed the Romans. It is hard to believe Jews make up something like this if they want other Jews to accept Jesus as Israel's Messiah.

JESUS AND WOMEN

To finish this chapter, we'll address one of the more misunderstood aspects of Jesus' life and ministry. Modern critics of the ignorant type think Christianity is fundamentally misogynistic. They are under the impression Christianity teaches women are inferior to men; however, it doesn't. In fact, it's just the opposite. The gospel stories present women in a way contrary to every cultural expectation of the time. The story of the "sinful" woman above is one of many examples.

We will be able to only scratch the surface; but remember as you read the gospels and Acts, and Paul's letters, the Jewish and pagan culture of the time was thoroughly patriarchal. In assumption and practice, men were superior and had all the authority. Women were at best second-class citizens with few legal rights. For the most part, their testimony wasn't even allowed in a court of law. Yet, some of Jesus' closest followers were women. He even invited women to sit at his feet while he taught, something that was unheard of at the time (e.g., Mary in Luke 10). Women just didn't do that in first century Jewish religious culture. Sitting and learning at a Rabbi's feet was for men; not only does Jesus let Mary do it, but he also reproves her sister Martha for being "worried and upset about many things," when she too should have been sitting at Jesus' feet. As we'll see in more detail in the chapter on Jesus' death and resurrection, women played a prominent role there as well. That's certainly something that wouldn't be included if you want people at the time, especially men, to buy what you're selling—unless it's true. Speaking of Jesus' death, Matthew (27) tells us at the cross:

> [55] Many women were there, watching from a distance. They had followed Jesus from Galilee to care for his needs.
> [56] Among them were Mary Magdalene, Mary the mother of James and Joseph, and the mother of Zebedee's sons.

Where were the men? They fled like the cowards they proved to be, save John. In apologetics this is called the criterion of embarrassment, meaning if something is embarrassing for what you're trying to prove, you don't include that, let alone make it up. In first century Jewish and pagan culture, you don't make men look bad and women look good, unless that's what really happened. In the narrative of Jesus' crucifixion, the men come off looking really bad, and the women really good.

Lastly, in John 4, we read what to the Jew of the time would have been a hard-to-swallow story of Jesus talking with a Samaritan woman. Jesus is resting by a well in a Samaritan town called Sychar in the middle of the day, and a woman came to draw water. He asked her for a drink, and she was shocked because Jews just don't talk to Samaritans like that, let alone a woman. Jews and Samaritans were hated enemies, so such an encounter would have been considered scandalous. When the disciples came back from the town with food, their response indicated as much:

> [27] Just then his disciples returned and were surprised to find him talking with a woman. But no one asked, "What do you want?" or "Why are you talking with her?"

Again, Jesus was doing the unexpected and the counter-cultural in the extreme. Isn't it funny and telling, that Jesus had something about him so intimidating to people even his disciples wouldn't ask, "What in the world are you doing talking to a Samaritan woman! Really, Jesus?" And not only that, but this is the first person to whom he reveals he is Israel's Messiah, and that to a woman who Jews saw as less than human. There are many other details in this story that sound authentic, that have verisimilitude in spades. It took a long time; but far from being anti-woman, Jesus began the transformation of the ancient view of women, to the modern. Without him nothing would have changed, and women would have remained not far above slaves in the social pecking order. Now we'll see how the supernatural adds to the credibility of the gospel narratives.

CHAPTER SEVEN
THE MIRACLES OF JESUS AND THE APOSTLES

Since the Enlightenment, biblical miracles have been the primary stumbling block for many to accept the Bible as true history. This skepticism took off in the 17th century and grew into full flower in the 20th. German theologian Rudolph Bultmann (1884-1976), one of the most influential New Testament scholars in the last century, bluntly conveys this mindset:

> It is impossible to use electric light and the wireless and to avail ourselves of modern medical and surgical discoveries, and at the same time to believe in the New Testament world of spirits and miracles.[1]

The truth is the contrary: Miracles in the Bible lend *more* credibility to the narrative, not less. Far from being difficult to believe, the way miracles are portrayed makes accepting them as historical much easier than the claim they are made up. The skeptic, by contrast, claims we all know miracles can't happen. I contend we know no such thing!

Bultmann's assertion, typical of skeptics, is a quintessential example of begging the question, which contrary to modern usage doesn't mean "raising the question." This logical fallacy is as simple to understand as is its widespread use. Without getting into the Greek and Latin origins of the concept, it basically means assuming what you're trying to prove, and is a form of circular reasoning. So, for our purposes, a skeptic *assumes* naturalism and that miracles cannot occur; therefore when they read about miracles in the Bible, they conclude the stories must have been made up. C.S. Lewis in the introduction to his book *Miracles* explains the obvious, that what he calls "the philosophical question" must be addressed first before we come to the text. If we exclude the supernatural, we'll conclude the miracles are not real. Such begging the question regarding miracles means people refuse to take seriously the evidence of the biblical text itself. Lewis states:

> It is no use going to the texts until we have some idea about the possibility or probability of the miraculous. Those who assume that miracles cannot happen are merely wasting their time by looking into the texts: we know in advance what results they will find for they have begun by begging the question.[2]

And boy has there been a lot of time wasting over the last 250 years! Christians, and any honest observer, won't do that. If God is posited as a real possibility, instead of rejecting him a priori (made before or without examination) as the question beggars do, then evidence pointing to the miraculous can be accepted with integrity.

Most scholars and historians today accept the gospels as essentially historical, except for the miracle stuff. That is completely arbitrary. How can they accept the Jesus who delivered the Sermon on the Mount, or the Jesus who tussled with the Pharisees, or who ate with tax collectors and sinners, but reject the Jesus who walked on water or fed thousands with a few loaves and fishes? There is no rational reason to accept the former and reject the latter. It is pure question-begging, anti-supernatural bias of the highest order! Those who argue for a non-supernatural Jesus (as do almost all critical biblical scholars for the last several hundred years) should be taken with more than a little skepticism. What makes the miracles so credible is how they are portrayed as a natural part of the narrative, not at all like legends and myths, but as straight forward eyewitness accounts. The gospels and Acts read like history not fiction, including the miracles; note how muted and matter of fact the miracle narratives are. They are all that way, which lends to their credibility.

A last point to buttress our case that the gospels and Acts are reliable eyewitness accounts are the geographical, archeological, and historical details. Geisler and Turek in *I Don't Have Enough Faith to Be an Atheist* lay out just how reliable:

> Classical scholar and historian Colin Hemer chronicles Luke's accuracy in the book of Acts verse by verse. With painstaking detail, Hemer identifies 84 facts in the last 16 chapters of Acts that have been confirmed by historical and archeological research... [K]eep in mind that Luke did not have access to modern-day maps or nautical charts.

They list all 84 facts, and it is stunning. Legends and myths don't read like this; and as I've said, modern historical fiction didn't exist in the ancient world. Next, they offer corroborating evidence for the historicity of the miracles: "Luke reports a total of 35 miracles in the same book in which he records all 84 of these historically confirmed details." Then, they ask a rhetorical question which is a challenge to the skeptic:

> Why would Luke be so accurate with the trivial details like wind directions, water depths, and peculiar town names, but not be accurate when it comes to important events like miracles?[3]

The only possible reason skeptics deny the veracity of the miracles is bias. Geisler and Turek do the same with the gospel of John and get the same results. It's much easier to believe the miracles happened.

THE NATURE OF BIBLICAL MIRACLES

We can't consider all of Jesus' miracles; but as elsewhere in the book, my goal is to help you look at all of them differently, with an eye to verisimilitude. Why, as we're reading the text, does it read as if it could have happened just as it's written? What is it about the story that lends it that feeling of *realness*, gives it credibility, as if it couldn't or wouldn't have been made up? These are crucial questions because the skeptics and critics insist that all or much of it was. I would argue, the burden of proof is greater for them than for we who trust the eyewitness accounts.[4] Understanding the nature of biblical miracles is also imperative if we're to accurately judge what the text claims it is, eyewitness historical accounts.

Biblical miracles are not magic. Their purpose is never to display raw power but to move forward God's redemptive purposes in history. That's why they are so rare in biblical history, which might surprise those who've never read the Bible. Miracles cluster around three significant redemptive periods, each affirming the message that God works in history to save His people. The first is the Exodus, and the events surrounding it. Another six or seven hundred years would pass before miracles occurred again in Israel, with the rise of the first prophets, Elijah and Elisha, in the 9th century BC. One might think the prophets who follow performed miracles as well, but that was not the case. Even John the Baptist, the great forerunner of the Messiah who is compared to Elijah, did not perform miracles. It seems he would be the perfect person to utilize miracles to support his message, and an invented John the Baptist likely would have; but what we read in the gospels is the real history of the real Baptist—no miracles. The third cluster of miracles would surround the greatest miracle worker in biblical history, Jesus of Nazareth, and his first followers.

TURNING WATER INTO WINE

In the gospel of John, we are introduced in the most unlikely of ways to Jesus the miracle worker. Having run out of wine at a wedding, Jesus' mother asks him to help so the wedding planners wouldn't be embarrassed (John 2); and he did. He turned water into wine, which does seem a bit like magic. What's the point of the hero being pressured by his mother into doing something he says he's clearly not ready to do? He tells her, "My time has not yet come." Far from magic, there is deep symbolic significance to the event. Jesus decided to use jars normally used for Jewish ceremonial washing and cleansing the body to prepare for worship. We'll remember later in his ministry Jesus declaring wine to be the symbol of a new covenant in his blood. Human efforts such as cleansing with water would no longer be relevant in a relationship to a holy God, but a mighty work of God on our behalf would be. There were six jars signifying the number of incompleteness in biblical numerology, while seven is the number of perfection. Jesus is bringing a New Covenant which the writer to the Hebrews tells us is superior to the Old, and this story gives us a hint at what's to come.

Jesus told the servants to fill the jars to the brim, each holding, according to John, 20 to 30 gallons. That's a lot of wine! I found a gallons-to-bottles of wine converter on the internet; and if the lower number is accurate, that is still almost 600 bottles of wine! That's almost funny. Wasn't Jesus concerned that the guests were already a little tipsy? Obviously not! Our God is no miser when it comes to celebrating a wedding feast, as no doubt we'll experience at the wedding feast of the Lamb in eternity. Maybe God had that in mind when he allowed this story to become part of His redemptive revelation to His people. And this wasn't just any old cheap swill. The master of the banquet, the guy running the show, had no idea where the wine came from; and he called the bridegroom aside and said, "Everyone brings out the choice wine first and then the cheaper wine after the guests have had too much to drink; but you have saved the best till now." Does this not read real! Would God in human flesh create cheap wine? Obviously not!

MIRACLES AND JESUS' AUTHORITY

The Synoptic Gospels (Matthew, Mark, and Luke) take a bit of a different tack than John, who builds his story around seven "signs" of Jesus or that which serves to confirm or authenticate his Messianic claims. John, who writes later to a primarily non-Jewish audience, established at the beginning who Jesus was as the divine Word of God;

and his works and teaching substantiate that throughout his ministry. Jesus' first miracle in John is low key (only his disciples and mother know about it), while in the Synoptics, Jesus comes out metaphorically swinging: Everyone knows of his many miracles. Only later in the story at the transfiguration do we find confirmation that he is the divine Son of God (Matt. 17, Mark 9, Luke 9). Skeptics claim that miracles are an add on (because of their materialist assumptions, they have to be), and that it was later writers who added them to make the case for Jesus as a divine being. Quite to the contrary, Jesus' miracles are so integral to the story, so necessary to the narrative, there would be no story worth telling without them in the first place.

Jews knew their history very well and how rare miracles were, and that God used them in quite specific, limited ways to prove His work among them. Initially, most Jews responded to Jesus' miracles as evidence that he came from God. Alfred Edersheim, himself a Jewish Christian scholar of the 19th century, argues how important it is that we look at the miracles from their perspective and time, not ours. They would have expected God to perform miracles to prove His working among them:

> It may therefore safely be asserted, that to the men of that time no teaching of the new faith would have been real without the evidence of miracles.[5]

In other words, people didn't decide Jesus was divine (Jews would *never* do that), and then attach miracles to him. It was the miracles that eventually persuaded them to believe he was divine *after* he rose from the dead. There was nothing in their Bible nor in the writings of the previous 400 years (the intertestamental period) to prompt first century Jews to look for a miracle-working Messiah, but miracles were required for them to believe a Messiah as unlikely as Jesus came from God. Nobody would have made up the miracles later, because the Jews would have needed miracles to be open to a divine Jesus in the first place.

Without any birth narrative, Mark's gospel dives right into Jesus' ministry. After being baptized by John and calling his first disciples, Jesus goes to Capernaum and amazes the crowds with his teaching. They'd never heard anything like this from their teachers of the law. Just then, a man in the synagogue possessed by an evil spirit cries out:

> [24] "What do you want with us, Jesus of Nazareth? Have you come to destroy us? I know who you are—the Holy One of God!"
>
> [25] "Be quiet!" said Jesus sternly. "Come out of him!" [26] The unclean spirit shook the man violently and came out of him with a shriek.
>
> [27] The people were all so amazed that they asked each other, "What is this? A new teaching—and with authority! He even gives orders to unclean spirits and they obey him." [28] News about him spread quickly over the whole region of Galilee.

Although Satan and the demonic were not unknown in the Old Testament, there is nothing like the demon possession we see throughout the gospels. Exorcism and casting out demons were also not unknown in first century Palestine among the Jews, but nothing like Jesus had ever been seen, especially the way demons reacted to him. F.F. Bruce gives us the reason that demons are unique features in the ministry of Jesus:

> The demon-possession which forms so prominent a feature of the gospel narrative is particularly rife because the kingdom of evil realizes that the advent of the divine kingdom confronts it with a mortal threat which must muster all its powers to resist.[6]

Up to the time of Jesus, Satan and his minions could do their work in the dark, so to speak, underground where they returned after his death and resurrection. God to some degree has given over this fallen world to Satan, but supernatural manifestations of his diabolical rule are rare (he's much more dangerous when people don't believe he exists). When Jesus came, it was all hands on the Satanic deck, and God gave them enough leash so Jesus could prove his authority and power over the dark forces of evil in the heavenly realms (Eph. 6:12). It might make us wonder, how would the writers of the gospels have invented this explosion of demonic activity if there was nothing like it before Jesus? Why didn't it continue after Jesus? Or in Acts, or in the lives of the early church fathers. Demonic activity like this is unique to the life and ministry of Jesus, and further evidence of the authenticity of the narrative.

JESUS' SPECIAL RELATIONSHIP TO WATER AND NATURE

Nothing is more absurd to the skeptic than Jesus' walking on water or stilling a storm just by his command. Impossible, so they tell us. However, the way in which these stories are told is powerful evidence for their truth. We'll first consider the latter (Matt. 8, Mark 4, and Luke 8). The details are similar in each telling. Jesus gets into a boat with his disciples and tells them they are going to go to the other side of the lake (of Galilee). Obviously exhausted, Jesus falls asleep while a furious storm comes up. Terrified, the disciples wake Jesus and plead with him to save them. Jesus' reply as Matthew reports it is priceless:

> [26] He replied, "You of little faith, why are you so afraid?"
> Then he got up and rebuked the winds and the waves, and
> it was completely calm.

Are you kidding me? How could they *not* be afraid? A raging storm, on a dark night, in a small boat in the middle of a large body of water is the *perfect* recipe for terror. But Jesus is as cool as a cucumber. Mark reports another question they ask in the midst of the squall: "Teacher, don't you care if we drown?" In a way that's amusing. Didn't Jesus say before they even got into the boat, "Let's go over to the other side of the lake?" Yes, in fact he did. He didn't say, we're going to the middle of the lake to drown. I guess when Jesus says something, he means it, storm or no storm. After calm returns, the disciples' response is even more priceless than before:

> ^{27} The men were amazed and asked, "What kind of man is this? Even the winds and the waves obey him!"

So let me get this right. They are terrified during the storm when they think they're going to die, and now they're terrified of the guy who saved their lives? The answer, and its implications, must have been troubling to say the least. The portrayal of the story has verisimilitude in spades.

There are wonderful spiritual lessons to take from this, but as you know by now that's not my goal. I want to know if this really happened. If it didn't, the spiritual lessons are worthless. If it didn't really happen, then Jesus wasn't who he said he was; and whoever made up this story is a liar. In this case we would have roughly a dozen liars. Then, are we to believe they all made it up, and continued to stick to the story even when they all knew it wasn't true? We have only two choices; either it happened, or it didn't. And it's an awfully odd story to make up if it didn't really happen. Imagine their getting to the other side of the lake and telling people what happened. They probably didn't, at least initially. It's too preposterous! They hardly believed it themselves. There is also nothing comparable in Israel's history. Even when Elijah called down fire from heaven in his encounter with the prophets of Baal (I Kings 18), he prayed to the Lord; and it was the Lord who did it, not Elijah. Here, Jesus himself is exerting power over nature by his mere word. God does such things, not man; yet here was a man doing it. No wonder they were freaking out. And to top it off, there was no expectation of the long-awaited Messiah having such power… none!

If this isn't crazy enough, imagine making up a story about Jesus and Peter walking on water (Matt. 14, Mark 6, and John 6). There is nothing remotely like this in biblical history. Instead of Jesus' getting in the boat with the disciples this time, he has them get in, and tells them he'll meet them on the other side. This, for those who deny it happened, has the same problem as the previous episode on the lake; it's a very strange thing to make up. Sometime after three in the morning on a wave-tossed and windy lake, the disciples see what they take as a ghost walking on the water; and it terrifies them. Who wouldn't be? They respond like real people encountering something unimaginable. Jesus tells them not to be afraid, it is him. In Matthew's account, impetuous Peter wants a little proof that it is in fact Jesus, so he asks Jesus to tell him to walk out to him on the water. Bad idea. As soon as he sees the wind and waves, he starts to sink. Terrified, Peter shouts, "Lord, save me!" Jesus' response fits a realistic narrative perfectly:

> [31] Immediately Jesus reached out his hand and caught him. "You of little faith," he said, "why did you doubt?"

Well, Jesus, because, you know, maybe people just don't walk on water? That reads so real. Then, Matthew writes something utterly un-Jewish: "Those who were in the boat worshiped him, saying, "Truly you are the Son of God." Worshiping a man, any man, even if he walks on water, is blasphemy. Mark has a little different take, saying that even though they were amazed, they really hadn't understood. Jesus had just previously fed more than five thousand people with a few loaves, but "they had not understood." Both accounts reflect perfect human ambivalence to something so inconceivable. I'll quote Alfred Edersheim again as to why it takes more faith to believe this is made up, than that it actually happened:

> Not only would the originations of this narrative… be utterly unaccountable—neither meeting Jewish expectancy, nor yet supposed Old Testament precedent—but, if legend it be, it seems purposeless and irrational. Moreover, there is this noticeable about it, as about so many of the records of the miraculous in the New Testament, that the writers by no means disguise from themselves or their readers the obvious difficulties involved.[7]

In other words, it doesn't read *at all* like legend or myth.

JESUS RAISES LAZARUS FROM THE DEAD

One of the most profoundly real stories in the gospels that doesn't read at all like legend or myth is Jesus bringing Lazarus back from the dead (John 11). What makes it so powerful is not only that Jesus could do such a thing, but his reaction to his friend's death as he stands in front of the tomb. It will be only moments before he brings him back to life, yet John tells us, "Jesus wept." Why in the world would Jesus cry? Why invent or add into the story Jesus' weeping when he's going to take care of the problem in mere moments? That's baffling, unless it really happened, but makes perfect sense when we realize how horrible, terrible, and cruel death is, especially to the one who created us to never experience something so disgusting and apparently final as death. Jesus wept at the aberration that death is to his created order.

We get an indication of Jesus' emotional state of mind when he sees others weeping, and John says "he was deeply moved in spirit and troubled." English doesn't do justice to the two Greek verbs that John used; but Jesus was angry and agitated, we might even say enraged. His tears come from a very deep place because as ugly as death is to us, only God can know its true horror. The story would be more comprehensible from a purely human perspective if Jesus doesn't cry, and doesn't become emotionally distraught in the face of a problem he's going to shortly fix. The story is far more credible read as true eyewitness history. If Jesus' reaction reads real, so does his bringing a man (dead four days) back to life just by his words, "Lazarus, come forth!"

I will address the miraculous again in the chapters on Jesus' birth, death, and resurrection, but space will not allow me to consider more examples here. Books could be written on our theme because Scripture is God's revelation, and as infinite as he is. So, I will briefly look at the miracles of the Apostles in Acts, specifically Peter and Paul, that further cements my contention the miraculous could not be made up.

ACTS AND THE APOSTLES

Miracles play the same role for the apostles as they did for Jesus: establishing their message is from God. As I mentioned above, this was expected by Jews who looked for God to confirm His work among His people. Sometime after Peter's first sermon in Acts 2 when about three thousand were added to their number, Luke tells us (v. 43), "Everyone was filled with awe at the many wonders and signs performed by the apostles." The first miracle described in Acts (3) by Peter affirms their proclamation of Christ is from God. As Peter and John are heading up to the Temple, a crippled beggar asks them for money but gets something else entirely. Peter says, "In the name of Jesus Christ of Nazareth, walk," and takes him by the hand to help him up; and he is completely healed. As he goes with them into the temple courts he's jumping around and praising God; and as people recognize him as the crippled beggar, "they were filled with wonder and amazement." I love the way Luke tells the story, that the beggar is holding on to Peter and John as people come running to see it for themselves. What does Peter do, tell them what great power he has? No, he says, "Why do you stare at us as if by our own power or godliness we had made this man walk?" Then, he begins to proclaim the resurrection and that it is only in Jesus' name this man was healed. Many believed, about 5,000 men according to Luke. As in the rest of the Bible, miracles in Acts further God's redemptive plans. Luke emphasizes this again (5:12), "The apostles performed many signs and wonders among the people." The miraculous isn't as prevalent as in the gospels; but once the authority of the Apostles had been established, it didn't need to be, and now we have their inscripturated, authoritative words in our Bibles.

Since I've included a chapter on the Apostle Paul, I won't take space here to address the miraculous in his life. I would only encourage you to read Acts and see how the miracles associated with his life and ministry have the same verisimilitude. Paul was the Apostle to the Gentiles, an especially tough job that went against not only his Jewish grain but that of all the other apostles. It was especially important for the Apostle to the Gentiles to have his ministry confirmed by displays of the power of God. In Acts 19 when Paul was in Ephesus for two years ministering mostly to Gentiles, "the word of the Lord spread widely and grew in power" throughout Asia. Luke tells us,

> [11] God did extraordinary miracles through Paul, [12] so that even handkerchiefs and aprons that had touched him were taken to the sick, and their illnesses were cured, and the evil spirits left them.

The miraculous in Paul's ministry is consistent with the miraculous in the rest of redemptive history. Luke, the careful chronicler, gives us every reason to trust his accounts are accurate and believable.

Now that we understand how the miraculous lends credibility to the narrative, in the next couple chapters we'll focus on how the non-miraculous in Jesus' life does the same.

CHAPTER EIGHT
JESUS' PERSONALITY— THE CONUNDRUM THAT WAS JESUS

Of any person in recorded history, Jesus would be the most difficult to invent, by far. Everyone wants a piece of Jesus, just not the whole Jesus found in the gospels. They take *some* of what's in the gospels to build a fictitious Jesus who suits their needs, isn't too offensive, and doesn't make unreasonable demands. This Jesus is, most importantly, non-judgmental (*Thou shalt not judge* is the only verse our secular neighbors seem to know) and positively lovey dovey, but completely arbitrary. He is not worth the paper he's written on. In every iteration of the partial Jesus, Hindu, Buddhist, Muslim, Enlightenment rationalism, and everything in between, he is a figment of human imagination. If we accept such a Jesus, we are submitting ourselves to some arbitrary human authority instead of the actual Jesus we discover in the gospels. C.S. Lewis made famous the trilemma argument,[1] either reject Jesus as a fraud or charlatan, or a liar, but let us not pretend he was some great moral teacher. He did *not* leave us that option.

THE DIFFICULT AND UNPREDICTABLE JESUS

As we previously discussed, Jesus was not the Messiah pious Jews in the first century expected. A tough one to figure out, he often confused, intimidated, surprised, angered, or frustrated those who encountered him—mostly he was a conundrum. My favorite cinematic portrayal of the conundrum Jesus, and one of the most biblically faithful, is Franco Zeffirelli's 1977 miniseries *Jesus of Nazareth*. His Jesus is a mystery to everyone—friends and foes alike. Even in our age when fiction has been a common art form for several hundred years, he would still be a very unlikely person to make up, let alone in an age before fiction. Myths and legends existed, but the gospels don't read anything like myths or legends. Instead, they read like straight-forward eyewitness history, which has proven to be a significant problem for critics and skeptics who want to explain away Jesus as mostly a figment of human imagination. That is a futile task, but they have been trying for a long time. Their efforts are not nearly as persuasive as the Jesus we find in the text of the gospels, as we'll see with the difficult and unpredictable Jesus.

THE UN-FAMILY-FRIENDLY JESUS

Out of the many examples, a few will be sufficient to give you a feel for how difficult it would be to make up the Jesus of the gospels. Let's start with a statement that completely contradicts the lovey dovey, let's-just-all-get-along Jesus. In Luke 12 we read what must have sounded preposterous to those who first heard it, especially Jews:

> [49] "I have come to bring fire on the earth, and how I wish it were already kindled! [50] But I have a baptism to undergo, and what constraint I am under until it is completed! [51] Do you think I came to bring peace on earth? No, I tell you, but division. [52] From now on there will be five in one family divided against each other, three against two and two against three. [53] They will be divided, father against son and son against father, mother against daughter and daughter against mother, mother-in-law against daughter-in-law and daughter-in-law against mother-in-law."

Wait. Jesus came to bring division not peace? Nobody at the time thought the Messiah's job would be to tear families apart. To a Jew, and their family-oriented culture, such a concept would be ridiculous and offensive. The Messiah was supposed to come and unite Israel against their oppressors, not mess up their families. Even today, if someone were biblically illiterate and read this passage, they would never say, "Oh yeah sure, that sounds just like Jesus!" They would likely respond that it is disturbing that anyone would teach such a thing. *That* is the real Jesus!

This is the same Jesus, mind you, who said in the Sermon on the Mount (Matt. 5-7), "Love your enemies, and pray for those who persecute you." He adds, "If you love those who love you, what reward will you get?" Let me get this straight. We are to alienate those who are closest to us, and love and pray for those who hate us. Got it. Only, that's nonsensical. It's hard to imagine someone making this up in the first century because it begins to make some sense only when you see the full scope of redemptive history encapsulated in our Bibles. Then, it's often difficult to accept and put into practice, or fully comprehend. The difficulty is to be expected when truth is addressed to those who by nature hate the truth. Hence, you wouldn't expect sinful, fallen people to make up ideas that run so contrary to their natures.

And Jesus practiced what he preached. I previously quoted the verses from Mark 3 (20, 21) where his family thinks he is "out of his mind." Not only does his family think he's nuts, in the very next sentence we read that the teachers of the law think he's possessed by the devil! A little later in that same chapter, Jesus' mother and brothers send someone into the house to get him. Ignoring them he asks, "Who are my mother and brothers?" Pointing around he says, they are who do God's will. This reads so strangely, especially in that culture, it must be real.

PETER TURNS INTO SATAN!

From a human perspective, a truly bizarre incident of the difficult, unpredictable Jesus is portrayed in one of my favorite scenes in *Jesus of Nazareth* (from Matt. 16, and Mark 8). Jesus has been doing and teaching remarkable things and asks his disciples who people think that he is.

Then he asks them point blank, and what about you, who do you say that I am? Peter (played wonderfully by James Farentino) declares him to be the Messiah, the Son of God. He is still Simon at that point, but Jesus tells him he is now Peter (which in Greek means rock), and that upon this rock (the declaration that he is the Messiah) he will build his church. Jesus tells him his Father in heaven has revealed this to him, and you must imagine Peter is feeling rather good about himself at this point. Jesus then immediately does something totally unexpected, of course, and tells them he is going to be killed in Jerusalem by the Jewish leaders. Imagine the heads of the disciples exploding at hearing that! They would have been utterly confused. How in the world could the Messiah be killed, let alone by his own people? The Messiah kills his enemies. He is *not* to be killed. Horrified at such a suggestion, impetuous Peter rebukes Jesus, "Never, Lord! This shall never happen to you!" Then we read these hard to fathom words, unless it was Jesus who really said them:

> [23] But he turned and said to Peter, "Get behind me, Satan! You are a stumbling block to me. You do not have in mind the things of God, but the things of man."

The rock has now become Satan? That is what you call whiplash. This scene is played wonderfully in *Jesus of Nazareth*. James Farentino's confused and dumbfounded reaction perfectly captures the conundrum Jesus. The gospels are silent on Peter's reaction, but the cinematic version must be close to the truth. We can also file this episode under the criterion of embarrassment. Inventing such a story about *the* leader of the early church, or that same leader denying three times that he even knew Jesus, wouldn't exactly lend credibility to the movement.

THE TRANSFIGURATION

One of the most unlikely-to-be-made-up stories about Jesus is the transfiguration (Matt. 17, Mark 9, Luke 9). Those who come to the text with an anti-supernatural bias will reject it out of hand and insist it was invented. By contrast, those who let the text speak for itself might come to a different conclusion.

A week or so after "Peter became Satan," Jesus took Peter, James, and John up a mountain to pray. Suddenly, Jesus was transfigured before them into a dazzling white, which the gospel writers have difficulty describing; and Moses and Elijah appeared with Jesus. Then, what must have sounded like thunder, they heard a voice from the cloud, "This is my Son, whom I love. Listen to him!" The disciples were terrified and confused and fell to the ground. Jesus told them they don't have to be afraid. After all, it was only a direct experience of Almighty God; what's to be afraid of!

This passage is redemptive-historical theological genius, and on that basis alone is a very improbable invention. Moses and Elijah represent everything the Jews held dear (the law and the prophets), and now God is saying Jesus has superseded them. This was a real-time supernatural display of what Jesus said throughout the Sermon on the Mount, "You have heard that it was said, but I tell you..." No pious Jew in the first century would *ever* have considered the Messiah in any way superior to the law and the prophets; they don't make this up, or the Jesus of the Sermon on the Mount. Later Jesus says something completely unexpected, especially to these disciples who had just seen a miraculous display of Jesus' divinity:

> [9] As they were coming down the mountain, Jesus gave them orders not to tell anyone what they had seen until the Son of Man had risen from the dead.

Mark says that Peter, James, and John kept the matter to themselves but discussed what "raising from the dead" meant. Jewish eschatology (the study of the end of time) was and is firmly rooted in a general resurrection of the dead. They were confused because no Jew expected any one person to be resurrected in the middle of history. I also love how they were too intimidated to ask Jesus directly what he meant, and we understand why Peter would especially be a bit gun shy. In so many ways Jesus was an inscrutable and confusing figure to his followers, evidence that the Bible is an accurate historical account of Jesus of Nazareth.

Alfred Edersheim has some persuasive insights about the Transfiguration:

> Few, if any, would be so bold as to assert that the whole of this history had been invented by the three Apostles, who professed to have been its witnesses. Nor can any adequate motive be imagined for its invention. It could not have been intended to prepare the Jews for the Crucifixion of the Messiah, since it was to be kept a secret till after his resurrection; and, after the event, it could not have been necessary for the assurance of those who believed in the resurrection, while to others it would carry no weight. [T]he special traits of this history are inconsistent with the theory of its invention.... The most untenable theory seems that which imputes intentional fraud to the narratives, or, to put it otherwise, non-belief on the part of the narrators of what they related.

What seems most strange is recounted only in Luke, who tells us that Jesus spoke with Moses and Elijah about "his departure, which he was about to bring to fulfillment in Jerusalem." Edersheim adds, "Anything more un-Jewish could scarcely be imagined than a Messiah crucified, or that Moses and Elijah should appear to converse with him on such a death!"[2] And remember, it was Jews writing this story, so they only tell it if it is true.

A SAMARITAN WOULD NEVER BE A JEWISH HERO

The idea of a "good Samaritan" as someone who helps others would have been an oxymoron to Jews during the time of Jesus. There was a long and contentious history between the Jews and Samaritans. So much so that they despised one another, each thinking they practiced Israel's true religion. So, when Jesus tells a parable (Luke 10) about a "good Samaritan," such a phrase was a contradiction in terms to a Jew, and offensive. A Jew would *never* have even considered making a Samaritan the hero of a story to teach a moral lesson on how to treat our neighbor, especially if he wanted to attract a following among Jews.

Jesus responds to a question from an expert of the law about how to inherit eternal life. Jesus' answer is to fulfill the greatest commandment: loving God, self, and neighbor. Because he wants to justify himself, he asks Jesus, "Who is my neighbor?" Jesus replies with a story. A Jewish man is going on a trip from Jerusalem to Jericho when he's overtaken by robbers, and severely beaten. The beauty of the story is that two Jews, a priest and Levite no less, avoid the battered man and refuse to help him; but a Samaritan passing by stops to help. That Samaritan, the expert of the law must admit, truly acted as the injured man's neighbor, and not the priest or Levite. We can imagine the Jews who heard Jesus tell the parable incredulously asking, "Who does this Jesus think he is, making Jewish religious leaders look bad, and a Samaritan look good!" Exactly.

HOW *NOT* TO WIN FRIENDS AND INFLUENCE PEOPLE

My mother often told me how a Jewish friend of hers used to say that Jesus was the greatest salesman who ever lived. However, I beg to differ. If you read the gospels, you'll find Jesus was a *terrible* salesman. He went out of his way to encourage people *not* to follow him; and human nature being what it is, a successful movement to change the world is *not* done this way. A normal, sinful, self-centered human being would never make this stuff up, ergo it had to come from the real Jesus who was the God-man, and Israel's Messiah, the Savior of the world. Only such a man would make these kinds of statements; in all recorded history, no one else has.

Let's start with the counter-intuitive notion of making the cross a "selling point." Twice Jesus uses the word to indicate what someone must do who wants to follow him (I'll quote from Matthew 10 and 16):

> [37] "Anyone who loves their father or mother more than me is not worthy of me; anyone who loves their son or daughter more than me is not worthy of me. [38] Whoever does not take up their cross and follow me is not worthy of me. [39] Whoever finds their life will lose it, and whoever loses their life for my sake will find it.

And…

> [24] Then Jesus said to his disciples, "Whoever wants to be my disciple must deny themselves and take up their cross and follow me. [25] For whoever wants to save their life will lose it, but whoever loses their life for me will find it.

For those who have lived after 2,000 years of Christian influence in Western history, it is difficult to grasp just how insane this must have sounded at the time. If you want to turn off people and discourage them from following you in the first century, this was a sure-fire way of doing it.

Not only is Jesus saying that loyalty to him trumps all other loyalties in our lives, but that anyone who follows him must deny themselves and suffer. And not just any suffering, but the kind of suffering that is comparable to the most horrific and shameful suffering the world has ever known. It is inconceivable that any Jew, or pagan for that matter, would make up something so gruesome as using bloody, sadistic torture unto death as a metaphor for loyalty. Nor would anybody at the time think of attributing such words to Jesus, unless he actually said them. And what kind of person even says such things? Maybe a sadistic monster could come up with something like it, but probably not. Death on a Roman cross was the most horrific thing imaginable to people at the time, as we'll discuss in the chapter on Jesus' death. In the mouth of Jesus, however, if he was in fact God who came in human flesh, the Savior of the world, then making demands of ultimate loyalty, self-sacrificing even unto death is perfectly reasonable. Only the real conundrum Jesus could have ever uttered such words.

To Jesus' closest followers he promised an especially easy going, prosperous life—a finding-your-best-life-now kind of life. Uh, not really. Not even close. In Matthew 10, we read the names of the 12 apostles as Jesus was about to send them out to preach to "the lost sheep of Israel." What do they have to look forward to? Being flogged in synagogues, betrayed by family members, hated by everyone, even death. In John 16 Jesus says to them, "The time is coming when anyone who kills you will think they are offering a service to God." Sign me up! What kind of person builds a movement to change the world with such promises? Certainly not a great moral teacher, nor could anyone envision such a teacher. Yes, Jews knew the prophets suffered for proclaiming the truth to Israel, but this was The Messiah—he and his followers would make *others* suffer.

Another terrible-salesman Jesus incident is known as the story of the rich young ruler (Matt. 19, Mark 10, Luke 18). An earnest rich man approached Jesus and asked, "Good teacher, what must I do to inherit eternal life?" Jesus answered, "No one is good—except God alone." On the surface his statement is confusing. (This is one of the "difficult sayings of Jesus," and I will address these in the next chapter.) Is Jesus implying that he's not good, and thus not divine, and just another sinner like everyone else? That seems to be the most straight-forward reading, but Scripture should never be interpreted in isolation. The overall view of the gospels affirms the divinity of Jesus, thus he is good; it stretches credulity to think someone put those words in Jesus' mouth.

Jesus continues with a recitation of a portion of the Ten Commandments to the rich young ruler who claims that he's kept all of them since he was a boy. Astounding his listeners, not least the rich man, Jesus replies: "You still lack one thing. Sell everything you have and give to the poor, and you will have treasure in heaven. Then come, follow me." This is another scene powerfully portrayed in *Jesus of Nazareth*. The young man is perplexed and can hardly believe what he's hearing. The gospels say he was downcast and went away sad. You can almost see him thinking, "What in the world does my wealth have to do with eternal life and keeping the commandments?" Next Jesus drops the bomb: "Truly I tell you, it is easier for a camel to go through the eye of a needle than for a rich man to enter the kingdom of God." His shocked disciples ask, "Who then can be saved?"

On this side of the history of Christianity it is hard to convey how upside-down such a teaching would have been to first century Jews. The reason is because of the history of monasticism. Monks made vows of poverty appear virtuous, and wealth suspicious, so we read this story and just pass on by. We don't realize that a normal first century Jew wouldn't teach such a thing. Wealth, like children, was a blessing from God, even though there are plenty of warnings in the Old Testament to not make wealth an idol. This verse in Deuteronomy 8 is a good example of why Jews understood wealth as blessing:

> [18] But remember the Lord your God, for it is he who gives you the ability to produce wealth, and so confirms his covenant, which he swore to your ancestors, as it is today.

Nothing was more important than Yahweh confirming his covenant with his people, and wealth was an indication of that. To say wealth would be an obstacle to attaining the blessing of God was perplexing to those who heard Jesus' teaching, since wealth was evidence of God's blessing. The only explanation for this story is that Jesus was absolutely unlike any Jew of his time. Alfred Edersheim says of Jewish attitudes, "We need scarcely here recall the almost extravagant language in which Rabbinism describes the miseries of poverty," and Edersheim knew the Rabbinic literature as well as anyone.[3] That's why his disciples asked a question we would never ask today, "Who then can be saved?" For them, wealth and salvation went together.

If Jesus wasn't so good at winning friends, he was especially good at creating enemies, primarily among the Jewish religious leaders. He had a knack for infuriating his pious opponents, and eventually gets himself killed because of it. The religion of Jesus and the religion of the Pharisees could not be more diametrically opposed, and Jesus seemed to know how to find exactly the right words to antagonize them. It was almost as if he were picking a fight, which he was. It is incomprehensible that the religiously-committed Jews who interacted with Jesus would have invented teaching that went counter to everything they had been taught all their lives—surely, they didn't.

THE ARGUMENT FROM JESUS

In apologetics there are many ways to go about defending Christianity, and arguing from some specific topic is an effective way to make the case. We can argue from design, or from evil, or from existence, or causation… or from Jesus. I agree with Tim Keller when he says, "Jesus himself is the main argument for why we should believe Christianity."[4] To say that Jesus was unusual, even apart from the miraculous, is a gross understatement. There have been many unusual people in history, but none who were so counter to every cultural and religious expectation of the time, not to mention how he affected people psychologically and emotionally. If the critics and skeptics are right, we would *have* to believe that all or most of what Jesus did and said was made up by people who clearly couldn't conceive of what they were supposedly making up. The gospel writers' inventing job would be even more difficult because of all those who had first- or second-hand knowledge of Jesus. As I argued previously, Jesus was way too popular to make up stories about him and expect these people to believe them.

In the oral culture of first century Judaism, all the stories and teaching about Jesus were first memorized, shared orally, and finally written down. In that pre-literate, pre-printed-word age, the Jewish people were fanatical about memorization. Jesus' closest followers had three years of daily contact and observation in which to commit his life and teaching to memory (some could have been written as well). J.P. Moreland is certainly right when he says, "Eyewitness apostolic control over the tradition is the best explanation for the emergence of a consistent, written portrait of Jesus."[5] A portrait that only fits if it is real.

Keller makes a poignant argument as well: "It is extraordinarily difficult to claim to be perfect and divine and then get the people who actually live with you to believe it. But Jesus did it."[6] Tom Gilson wrote an entire book about just this called *Too Good to be False*. He makes our point well:

> There's really just one good explanation for Jesus' character: *No one* made him up. No one could have. The stories must be true accounts of the real life lived by the most extraordinary person ever. He's too good to be false.[7]

To which we can all say, amen! If Jesus were a fraud, phony, or liar, or as some claim just a good moral teacher, those closest to him would surely never have died for him, but they did. No, everything points to him being a conundrum with one answer: Jesus was Israel's Messiah, the Son of God, Savior, and risen Lord.

CHAPTER NINE
JESUS' TEACHING

As we've seen, Jesus was continually doing the unexpected, and nowhere is this truer than in his teaching. We might think nothing could be more unexpected than his miracles, but they could be explained away. Even his enemies who admitted his miraculous powers insisted that power came from the devil. His teaching, though, would leave no doubt about his Messianic claims and their implications. It eventually got him crucified, the very last thing expected of Israel's 400-years-long-awaited Messiah. If it would have been unlikely for first century Jews to make up Jesus' miracles and his personality—as they were contrary to everyone's expectations—that is especially so for his teaching. By the time of Jesus, Jewish religion was in every aspect dictated by the Jewish religious professionals, Pharisees, Sadducees, and teachers of the law who are practically ubiquitous (160 references) in the gospels. They didn't get along so well with Jesus. We might ask, could what Jesus taught in the gospels be invented by Jewish people steeped in the Jewish religion of the time? His teaching in every way turned their religious world upside down. If Jesus wasn't someone outside of his time, how can what he taught and said be explained? Our good friend Alfred Edersheim makes the point commenting on the Sermon on the Mount:

> At the same time, it must carry to the mind, with almost irresistible force, the question whence, if not from God Jesus had derived his teaching, or how else it came so to

differ, not in detail, but in principle and direction, from that of all his contemporaries.[1]

We should take seriously what Edersheim is saying: not some of his contemporaries, but *all* of them. Critics will tend to ignore the pertinent issue: If his teaching *doesn't* come from God, where does it come from? They act as if ideas so contrary to *every* inclination of the day are not a problem for their assessment of Jesus as a mere human being. They've been insisting that for several hundred years it is not a problem at all. We can realistically put the burden of proof on them. Writing in the 19th century, Edersheim wasn't about to let them get away with it. He asks a similar question in the same context:

> Thus, there was, at the very foundation of religious life, absolute contrariety between Jesus and his contemporaries. Whence, if not from heaven, came a doctrine so novel as that which Jesus made the basis of his kingdom?[2]

There is no facile answer to this, as much as the skeptics and critics might like to think there is. And Jesus' teaching wasn't just novel, but completely contrary, as in upside down, inside out. Only in biblical hindsight can we now see how ingeniously it was the fulfillment of all that came before. That's why Jesus said to the disciples after his resurrection the entire Old Testament was about him, which couldn't possibly have come out of any other mouth than Jesus of Nazareth.

IT'S ALL OR NOTHING AT ALL: THE PROBLEM WITH PARTIAL JESUS

As I said in the last chapter, everyone wants a piece of Jesus; and this is especially hypocritically true about his teaching. People love the Jesus who associates with the outcasts of society, and teaches love and forgiveness; but they ignore the Jesus who teaches about hell. Unfortunately for them it's a package deal; one in the same Jesus taught both. But this arbitrary inconsistency doesn't stop people from using

Jesus to further their own ideological and religious agendas. A great example comes from a book I'm currently reading. The author speaks of "Christ's populist prose" that "was inevitably pitted against sophisticated religions." He states, "The few simple words he uttered seemed to have a universal and inherently uncontrollable strength such that their influence grew despite the obscurity of his life and death."[3] Exactly which "few simple words" would those be? And exactly how "populist" was his prose when he seemed to alienate almost everyone, and made it as difficult as possible to be his follower? As we saw in the last chapter, not very "populist" at all. And, however few his words, there was most definitely *nothing* simple about them at all! Such a distortion of Jesus is a common occurrence and terribly annoying. You can tell this author either knows nothing about Jesus' actual words recorded in the gospels, or more likely, he does what non-Christians always do, arbitrarily pick and choose which words of Jesus suit their taste.

As I said, the burden of proof must be on such people to justify their partial Jesus. We ought not to let them get away with it. Partial Jesus has been used for every movement and religion since Mohammed decided he could turn Jesus into a mere prophet while growing his bloody way into a new religion. We can't let them take fragments of him and pretend he's the real historical Jesus whose life, death, and resurrection—and yes, his teaching, all of it—was the basis of a new religion grown out of an incredibly old one. Any Jesus that doesn't consider *all* he said and did, every single bit of it, every word and syllable, is a phony Jesus. Here is a crucial point that bears repeating: Partial Jesus doesn't exist except in the minds of those who arbitrarily pick and choose bits and pieces of him for no rational or logical reason. It must be all or nothing at all! It's relatively easy to make up a partial Jesus; but the full Jesus, he's a real problem for the critics and skeptics.

THE FORGIVENESS OF SIN

I want to give readers a feel for how difficult it would be for Jews to make up the teaching of Jesus. No Jew who had ever lived up to that time, or since, would claim the authority to forgive the sin of *other* people but here was Jesus claiming just that. We're to believe Jews writing about Jesus would have thought it a good idea to make him a forgiver of sins, even though that's a prerogative of God alone, not to mention blasphemous? We see this play out in the story of the healing of the paralytic (Matt. 9, Mark 2, Luke 5).

In the last chapter I referenced the 1977 miniseries *Jesus of Nazareth*, and how well certain scenes portrayed the conundrum that was Jesus. The healing of the paralytic scene was certainly one of those, and I can imagine it happened something like Franco Zeffirelli staged it. Jesus was teaching a large crowd of people, including religious professionals who had come from all over Judea to hear him. Jesus' reputation preceded him; and in that day before modern medicine, he was in big demand as a healer. And he wasn't just healing one person here and there, he was healing everyone. Luke says just prior to our story, "[T]he news about him spread all the more, so that crowds of people came to hear him and be healed of their sicknesses." Imagine everyone's surprise when this specific healing didn't play out quite as they expected—as if Jesus ever did the expected.

Trying to fight their way through the crowd, some men couldn't find a way to bring their paralytic friend to Jesus for healing. Luke tells us what happened next: "They went up on the roof and lowered him on his mat through the tiles into the middle of the crowd, right in front of Jesus." How dramatic! Now what? Jesus had healed many people before, so the anticipation must have been palpable. Then Jesus, being Jesus, did something nobody could have imagined or predicted, much less invented:

> When Jesus saw their faith, he said to the paralytic, "Take heart, son; your sins are forgiven."

What? I'm sure it took a minute to register. All four gospel writers focus on the thoughts of the religious leaders who say among themselves, logically, "Why does this fellow talk like that? He's blaspheming! Who can forgive sins but God alone?" Exactly! So, Jesus confronts them with a rhetorical question that is in a way comical: "Which is easier: to say, 'Your sins are forgiven,' or to say, 'Get up and walk?'" Seriously, this is way too perfect to have been made up. Anyone can *say* anything, so it's easy to say *both* of those things. The issue is who is doing the saying! Then to make his point, Jesus put his authority where his mouth was:

> [10] But I want you to know that the Son of Man has authority on earth to forgive sins." So he said to the man, [11] "I tell you, get up, take your mat and go home." [12] He got up, took his mat and walked out in full view of them all.

Minds were appropriately blown. Jesus taught by doing. Critics have complained for eons that Jesus didn't come right out and say, "Yo, hey everyone, look at me, I'm God. You know, Yahweh, Old Testament and all that." How effective would that have been? As it was, slowly teaching and showing them over three years he was in fact God in human flesh still got him killed. If he just declared it walking out of the river Jordan after John baptized him, he may not have lasted three weeks.

THE HARD SAYINGS OF JESUS

The so-called hard sayings of Jesus would be especially challenging for first century Jews to invent. One aspect of these are his ethical teachings. Craig Blomberg states, "Much of Jesus' ethical instruction as portrayed in the gospels is so challenging that it is unlikely that it would have been invented."[4] Why would the gospel writers make up teaching that would not only make their lives more difficult, but even be impossible to attain? The Sermon on the Mount (Matt. 5-7) fits that bill perfectly. Jesus prefaced his ethical instruction with words his hearers must have found confusing:

[17] "Do not think that I have come to abolish the Law or the Prophets; I have not come to abolish them but to fulfill them."

After 2,000 years of Christian history, we read these words and barely blink; but think about what Jesus is saying and ask yourself, "Would any Jew at the time have put these words in Jesus' mouth? How could any Jew say such a thing? Is Jesus really claiming he, personally, can fulfill all of it?" There is profound theological meaning in Jesus' words, but on the surface, it would be ridiculous for any human being to make such a claim, unless the one making the claim could pull it off. No human being, let alone a first century Jewish human being, believes anyone could fulfill every ethical demand of the Jewish religion—or even more crazy, could fulfill everything every prophet of Israel predicted. Let's see what Jesus has in mind.

- Don't even be angry with your brother, let alone murder.
- Even looking at a woman lustfully is adultery.
- No divorce except for marital unfaithfulness.
- Do not resist an evil person.
- Love your enemies and pray for those who persecute you.
- Give, pray, and fast in secret.
- Do not store up treasures on earth but in heaven.
- Do not judge others.

And right in the middle of it all he says, "Be perfect, therefore, as your heavenly Father is perfect." No problem! The only reason this teaching of Jesus doesn't shock us is because we're too familiar with it. Love your enemies? No person in the ancient world where power controlled everything, where might made right, would say such a thing. We could take apart everything Jesus said to show how contrary it was to the Jewish and pagan mentality of the time. Everything about Jewish religious teaching at the time was external conformity, not inward transformation. The standards of the Jewish law were difficult to keep, but everyone assumed they were doable. This understanding of their religion is what led to the distinction between those who were religious and kept the law, and "sinners."

EAT MY FLESH AND DRINK MY BLOOD

There are many more difficult sayings and teachings of Jesus we could focus on, but one scenario is surely the most bizarre and incomprehensible, unless it came from Jesus, the divine Son of God. Not being a scholar and having only a cursory knowledge of ancient legends and myths, I don't know if there is anything comparable to what Jesus says in John 6. We're not dealing here with legends and myths, however, but with Jewish people in a thoroughly Jewish context. Could a Jewish person, not the divine Son of God, say something like this without being considered a lunatic? Even more improbable, could someone Jewish come up with these sayings, and attribute them to the Jewish Messiah? Before I address this, I will quote Jewish historian Geza Vermes as an example of those who ignore the difficulties of such passages. He says, "No objective and enlightened student of the Gospels can help but be struck by the incomparable superiority of Jesus." He then quotes from another Jewish author:

> In his ethical code there is a sublimity, distinctiveness and originality in form unparalleled in any other Hebrew ethical code; neither is there any parallel to the remarkable art of his parables.

Then Vermes adds:

> Second to none in profundity of insight and grandeur of character, he is in particular an unsurpassed master of the art of laying bare the inmost core of spiritual truth and of bringing every issue back to the essence of religion, the existential relationship of man and man, and man and God.[5]

There is a lot of fly food in those sentences made to smell like roses. The only way anyone can make such breathtakingly inane comments is by dealing with a partial Jesus, a Jesus who doesn't say things like *eat my flesh and drink my blood*. To harbor such thoughts, a person would have to ignore a large portion of what Jesus actually said according to the gospels. The trilemma we've discussed is spot on, either the Jesus who says these things is Lord, or he is a lunatic, or a liar. The Jesus of Vermes is not an option. So, what exactly does Jesus say? First,

> I am the bread of life. Whoever comes to me will never go hungry, and whoever believes in me will never be thirsty.

A merely great ethical teacher does not say such things. Then, he adds these bewildering words:

> [51] I am the living bread that came down from heaven. Whoever eats this bread will live forever. This bread is my flesh, which I will give for the life of the world."

Let's get this straight, Jesus. You are this living bread, which is your flesh, and we're supposed to eat it? No wonder the people hearing this were disturbed. In case there is any doubt:

> [53] Jesus said to them, "Very truly I tell you, unless you eat the flesh of the Son of Man and drink his blood, you have no life in you. [54] Whoever eats my flesh and drinks my blood has eternal life, and I will raise them up at the last day. [55] For my flesh is real food and my blood is real drink. [56] Whoever eats my flesh and drinks my blood remains in me, and I in them. [57] Just as the living Father sent me and I live because of the Father, so the one who feeds on me will live because of me. [58] This is the bread that came down from heaven. Your ancestors ate manna and died, but whoever feeds on this bread will live forever."

Understandably, his disciples respond: "This is a hard teaching. Who can accept it?" I don't know about hard, but it sure is strange, especially if Jesus is merely a Jewish religious guy trying to get followers. It's even more bizarre if one of those followers made up these words and put them in Jesus' mouth. It prompts us to ask, what kind of demented person would make up such stuff? An exercise I suggested previously makes my point. Take this passage out of its biblical context, don't tell who said it, and then let a secular person read it. What do you think their response would be? I'm not sure I need to answer that. Even in context, in real time, spoken by Jesus of Nazareth, it didn't get a rousing welcome: "From this time many of his disciples turned back and no longer followed him."

THE WAY, THE TRUTH, AND THE LIFE

The claim to exclusivity made Christians and Christianity persona non grata in the ancient world every bit as much as it does in our own. It was "controversial" from the start; and people, especially those in power, just wanted it to go away. This claim to be the one and only true way to God wasn't the idea of Christians, as critics might claim, but came directly from the teaching of Jesus of Nazareth. As I stated previously, nobody expected the Messiah Jesus turned out to be. Nobody would have imagined him as the sole conduit to God, as if a human being could ever perform such a role. There were mediators in the Old Testament—prophets, priests, and kings—but one person could certainly never perform all three offices until Jesus claimed he did. The way, truth, and life reference comes from John 14, which is an excellent example of the conundrum Jesus. He says some of the most astounding things in this passage that are very difficult to believe unless they are true. I find it far easier to believe they were spoken by a Jesus who was exactly who he said he was.

First, Jesus says his disciples should believe, or trust, in him the same way they trust in God. Any Jew who asserted such a thing would be instantly stoned, as almost happened to Jesus numerous times. He then tells them his Father's house has many rooms or dwelling places;

and he is going there to prepare a place for them, then come back and take them to be with him. Seriously, who would say something like this? Someone who, if a mere man, had delusions of grandeur to a psychotic degree. The only other option was that Jesus was telling the truth. Next, he says something typically Conundrum Jesus that they don't get: "You know the way to the place where I am going." Appropriately, Thomas the doubting apostle asks, "Lord, we don't know where you are going, so how can we know the way?" It's always amusing how clueless his closest followers were, and the gospels never have a problem presenting them that way. Jesus answers with a world transforming statement I would argue could never, ever have been made up by a Jew unless it were true and said by Jesus himself:

> [6] Jesus answered, "I am the way and the truth and the life. No one comes to the Father except through me. [7] If you really know me, you will know my Father as well. From now on, you do know him and have seen him."

Let that sink in for a bit. Those who have no knowledge of the Torah (the first five books of the Bible) and the Jewish religion, would have no idea how radical these statements were. In Exodus 33, Moses had asked Yahweh to show him his glory, and was given the answer, "No one may see me and live." And now here is Jesus of Nazareth, a mere carpenter from Galilee, telling his followers that, since they've seen him, they've seen God himself! His listeners could have easily thought he was deranged. Critics and skeptics have a real problem explaining this coming from a merely human Jesus. Or they may say Jesus was a great guy and all, super wonderful moral teacher, and sure he said a few crazy things; but all things considered, he's an inspiration for moral goodness. Dude! Morally good teachers don't say such things; they are wrapped in a white coat in a round room. This is yet another example as seen all through the gospels where the critics and skeptics can't have it both ways. Either Jesus was who he said he was, or he was one of the most deceptively evil human beings who ever lived. I'm going with the former because nobody, except some of the Jews who had him killed, thought he was the latter.

THE FIRST WILL BE LAST, AND THE LAST WILL BE FIRST

It's unfair I can pick only one more example of how upside down and impossible it was to make up Jesus' teaching, but I must exercise self-control.

I will focus on a few passages in Matthew where Jesus inverts the power dynamics of the day. First, however, I want to quote Tim Keller who does a good job capturing the subversive and countercultural nature of Jesus' life and teaching:

> [The] pattern of the cross means that the world's glorification of power, might and status is exposed and defeated. On the cross Christ wins through losing, triumphs through defeat, achieves power through weakness and service, comes to wealth via giving all away. Jesus Christ turns the values of the world upside down… This upside-down pattern so contradicts the thinking and practice of the world that it creates an 'alternative kingdom,' and alternative reality, a counterculture among those who have been transformed by it.[6]

I previously mentioned Tom Holland, an historian of the ancient world who wrote a book called *Dominion: How the Christian Revolution Remade the World*; and he makes Keller's point over the vast sweep of history. He argues Jesus' teaching is not shocking to us because it has so completely transformed Western civilization and culture that we take it for granted. The reason people think it could be made up is because Christian morality founded on the teaching of Jesus is the basic morality of Western civilization. Before you laugh, realize that without Christianity slavery would still be a commonly accepted practice; concern for the poor, the sick, and the marginalized would be rare; hospitals or universal education would likely not exist; human rights, an oxymoron;

and equality would be unknown (all concepts inconceivable to ancient people before Christianity). Jesus could not have been a product of the ancient world, Jewish or pagan; he transformed it.

One of the ways Jesus accomplished this colossal transformation was his approach to children. For example, he praised the Father (Matt. 11) for hiding his teaching from the wise and learned and revealing it to little children, even saying this was the Father's "good pleasure." Later in Matthew (18), his disciples come to him with a question typical of human kingdoms: "Who, then, is the greatest in the kingdom of heaven?" We don't know what kind of answer they were expecting, but typical of the unexpected Jesus, what he said must have been shocking:

> [2] He called a little child to him, and placed the child among them. [3] And he said: "Truly I tell you, unless you change and become like little children, you will never enter the kingdom of heaven.
>
> [4] Therefore, whoever takes the lowly position of this child is the greatest in the kingdom of heaven.

You can hear them thinking, "What kind of strange kingdom that would be! A kingdom is ruled by strong men who exert power, not by children."

Later (Matt. 20) the mother of James and John asks Jesus if her sons can sit at his left and right hand in his kingdom, ultimate positions of authority, and thus power. Jesus again replies in a way no one could have imagined, or invented:

> [25] Jesus called them together and said, "You know that the rulers of the Gentiles lord it over them, and their high officials exercise authority over them. [26] Not so with you. Instead, whoever wants to become great among you must be your servant, [27] and whoever wants to be first must be your slave— [28] just as the Son of Man did not come to

be served, but to serve, and to give his life as a ransom for many."

Just prior to this, Jesus told a parable of the workers in the vineyard, and ended it with, "So the last will be first, and the first will be last." Let me get this right, Jesus. You're saying the way to go up is to go down, and the way to go down is to go up? To first century people that was ludicrous. Those who think these are wonderful sentiments from a great moral teacher have no clue the only reason they think that is because of Jesus! His teaching, though, would mean nothing if he were not who he said he was—had he not been conceived by the Holy Spirit as the God-man, died on a Roman cross, and rose from the dead. To these seemingly impossible historical facts we go next.

CHAPTER TEN
JESUS' BIRTH AND DEATH

Having lived 2,000 years in a Western civilization that was created in large part because of the birth, death, and resurrection of Jesus of Nazareth, it is hard for us to grasp the utter improbability of these events. Christmas and Easter have lulled many people into thinking they could *easily* be made up; and as I've mentioned previously, the primary reason many people might believe that is a matter of a bias against miracles, rather than available historical evidence. Virgin birth and resurrection are miracles; therefore, they can't happen. Without having such a bias, however, we can come to the text in its ancient Jewish context and see how inconceivable it would have been to the Jews. No Jew could conceive God becoming man, this man being the Messiah, this Messiah dying the most ignominious death imaginable on a Roman cross, and then coming back from the dead three days later. Michael Green puts it this way:

> If you had looked the whole world over for more stony and improbable soil in which to plant the idea of an incarnation you could not have done better than light upon Israel![1]

That is just for Jesus' birth. For his death and resurrection, there is no soil, just rocks. I will address the resurrection in the next chapter.

A VIRGIN CONCEPTION AND BIRTH

Put aside popular images of Christmas, cute little baby Jesuses in mangers, Mary and wise men, and shepherds in the fields. As I've said numerous times, we're just too familiar with the stories to appreciate how shocking they are. There is nothing cute about a poor young pregnant peasant girl (probably not much into her teenage years) and her humble carpenter husband traveling roughly 90 miles from Nazareth to Bethlehem by foot or donkey, we're not told. We don't know how far along Mary was in her pregnancy, but the trip had to be miserable. Is this really the way God himself enters the world as a man? In hindsight, theologically, it's brilliant—the humility, the identification with the poor and powerless, God relating to the apex of his creation by becoming one of them, the necessity of a Messiah being sinless, untainted with the guilt of Adam's sin so he could pay the price of guilt for that sin.

Religious Jews of the first century, however, didn't have the benefit of such hindsight. Since the critics insist a virgin conception and birth can't happen, we are led to the inescapable question: Could such Jews have invented the story of a virgin birth in which God becomes man? Which leads to asking another one: Where would such an idea have come from if it were not true? What antecedents in Jewish history or culture or religion would have made such fiction possible? According to Jewish historian Geza Vermes there were none:

> [N]o biblical reason existed for inventing a virgin birth since it was not, and never had been, believed in biblical or inter-Testamental Judaism that the Messiah would be born that way.[2]

But, as a Jew, I'm certain Vermes believed Jesus was *not* conceived and born to a virgin, and so had to believe it was in fact invented. *That* I find hard to believe.

It is also not just a virgin bearing a child that makes the story so incredible, but the circumstances of the birth of the Jewish Messiah given the expectations of who this Messiah would be. A king like David, born to peasant parents in a smelly stable in the middle of nowhere, and with smelly shepherds as the first eyewitnesses? From a merely human perspective the king of the Jews and the king of the universe would surely not be born in such an environment. Alfred Edersheim, who knew the Jewish world of the first century as well as anyone, gives us an idea of how improbable it would be:

> [A] Messiah, the offspring of a Virgin in Galilee betrothed to a humble workman—assuredly, such a picture of the fulfillment of Israel's hope could never have been conceived by contemporary Judaism. There was in such a Messiah absolutely nothing—past, present, or possible; intellectually, religiously or even nationally—to attract but all to repel.
>
> [T]he circumstances… afford the strongest indirect evidence of the truth of this narrative. For, if it were the outcome of Jewish imagination, where is the basis for it in contemporary expectation? Would Jewish legend have ever presented its Messiah as born in a stable, to which chance circumstances has consigned his Mother? The whole current of Jewish opinion would run in the contrary direction.[3]

So much more could be said about the most consequential event in human history—the Creator of the universe becoming part of His creation through the birth canal of a young, Jewish, peasant woman. But I go back to something I've said over and over, and I hope you're getting tired of my saying it, because we must never forget it. Critics *insist* the Christmas story was all, or most or some of it, the product of human imagination, fiction invented to further a religious narrative. To them, making it up is easier to believe than that it actually happened because, well, virgins don't have babies! In fact, thinking it is fiction made up by first century Jews is much more difficult to believe. To Jews at the time, not only would the story have been inconceivable (in the true meaning of the word, unable to be conceived), it would have been repulsive to them. This is *not* how their Messiah was to be born, especially one conceived before his parents' marriage was even consummated.

JESUS, THE BASTARD CHILD

I'll never forget when I first heard the word bastard associated with Jesus in a sermon almost 40 years after I'd become a Christian. It struck me that I'd never really thought through the implications of that word related to Jesus. It used to mean an illegitimate child, because the child was born to parents who were not married. We're too "enlightened" today to use such a term to "stigmatize" a child through no fault of his own; and that's not a bad thing, but neither is stigmatizing birth outside of marriage. There was no ambivalence, however, in the first century. Having a child out of wedlock in a small rural village in Palestine was deeply problematic. In any such traditional context, specifically a very Jewish one, the child would likely receive the brunt of the abuse for flouting accepted cultural and religious norms. God never makes it easy, even for his own Son. First, let's briefly establish from the gospels that Jesus was in fact an illegitimate child.

The early church had to deal with accusations that Jesus had been born of adultery (a betrothal at the time was considered as binding as marriage), or even worse that Jesus was the result of a sexual relationship Mary had with a Roman centurion named Pantera. We get strong hints from the gospels as to why people at the time might have thought this. In Mark 6 Jesus is teaching in his hometown synagogue, and Mark tells us the people's response:

> "Where did this man get these things?" they asked. "What's this wisdom that has been given him? What are these remarkable miracles he is performing? [3] Isn't this the carpenter? Isn't this Mary's son and the brother of James, Joseph, Judas, and Simon? Aren't his sisters here with us?" And they took offense at him.

In a paternalistic Jewish culture not naming Jesus' father was telling. In every genealogy recorded in the Bible, including Matthew and Luke, never once is "the mother of" or "the son of the mother" used. The only time women are mentioned is in Matthew; and they are not paragons of moral virtue, except Mary, and even there Mary is only mentioned as being the wife of Joseph. Luke (2) in his genealogy doesn't even mention Mary, saying only about Jesus, "He was the son, so it was thought, of Joseph." Many of his contemporaries didn't believe Jesus was Joseph's biological son because the details of the betrothal and pregnancy would have been too well known to deny.

We also see this played out in John 8 and 9 in one of the many confrontations Jesus had with the Pharisees. In a debate about his divine authority, Jesus appeals to his Father to validate his testimony, and the Pharisees ask (8:19), "Where is your father?" As famous as Jesus was, the circumstances of his birth were likely well known, if not well understood. A little later in this contentious discussion (v.41), they say to Jesus, "We are not illegitimate children," possibly implying that he is. In chapter 9 (v. 29) to make the implication clearer, they say about Jesus, "as for this fellow, we don't even know where he comes from." Everyone knew Jesus was from Nazareth, so the reasonable implication from their statement is that nobody knew who his real father was.

We should wonder, who would make up a story about the divine Son of God, Israel's long-awaited Messiah, being a bastard? In hindsight we can see this is the only way the divine Son of God could be born as a man without sin. When Joseph took Mary home as his wife (Matt. 1:24), Jesus was formally adopted by Joseph, and became a legal and legitimate heir of Israel's Davidic lineage. Their neighbors and extended family in the small village of Nazareth didn't know that at the time, so knowing human nature I'm inclined to believe Jesus had a tough childhood, likely shared with his parents.

"CAN ANYTHING GOOD COME FROM NAZARETH?"

Speaking of Nazareth, you may remember these words from the first chapter of John when Philip introduces "Jesus of Nazareth" to Nathanael. We gather that this little backwater town didn't have the best of reputations. Of course, Israel's Messiah would come from such a town, right? Not exactly. I addressed this in the chapter on the Jewish Nature of Jesus' world, but it bears repeating here. The Jewish religion at the time of Jesus' birth was dominated by the Pharisees, which is the reason Nathanael responded the way he did. The Pharisees considered people from Galilee, where Nazareth was, not only culturally backward, but religiously inferior. "[T]he rabbinic portrait of the Northerner was a figure of fun, an ignoramus, or both. [F]or the Pharisees and the rabbis of the first and early second century AD the Galileans were on the whole boors."[4] If you want your Messiah to be respected and accepted, you don't make him come from Nazareth. Yet Nazareth—Jesus' hometown, that which defined him in the eyes of his contemporaries—was the place God chose as his hometown. Daniel Darling gets to the heart of Nathanael's question: "Why would I be interested in someone who comes from a part of the world that nobody respects?"[5] Exactly, and why Jesus the Messiah was almost certainly from Nazareth.

Regardless of where Jesus came from, his words and deeds made him impossible to ignore. The religious professionals certainly tried to discount and disregard him, but it didn't work. He became so popular that, near the end when they were looking for a way to arrest him, they were afraid of the people because they thought he was a prophet. Whatever anyone thought of Jesus, dying on a Roman cross was the very last thing that could happen to their long-awaited Messiah, until it did.

CRUCIFIXION AND DEATH

Of the many things difficult for Jews to invent, the crucifixion could reasonably be put at the top of the list. In the first century nobody, Jew or Pagan, would have seen a man dying on a cross as the least bit religious.

In the Roman world, according to Martin Hengel, crucifixion was such a horrific and disgusting business there is almost no mention of it in inscriptions. The cultured and literary of the time wanted nothing to do with it, and almost never mentioned it. He states:

> The heart of the Christian message, which Paul described as the 'word of the cross,' ran counter not only to Roman political thinking, but to the whole ethos of religion in ancient times and in particular the ideas of God held by educated people… A crucified messiah, son of God or God must have seemed a contradiction in terms to anyone, Jew, Greek, Roman, or barbarian, asked to believe such a claim, and it will certainly have been thought offensive and foolish.[6]

I could multiply quotes from Hengel's little book, but one more conveys the improbability of the shameful death of the Jewish Messiah on the cross being a Jewish invention:

> [T]he first Christian proclamation shattered all analogies and parallels to Christology which could be produced in the world of the time, whether from polytheism or from monotheistic philosophy.[7]

As offensive as it was to anyone at the time, it was especially so to Jews. To claim that God's own son would come to earth to specifically die on a Roman cross was beyond inconceivable. Tom Holland in his book *Dominion* puts it well:

> That such a god, of all gods, might have had a son, and that this son, suffering the fate of a slave, might have been tortured to death on a cross, were claims as stupefying as they were, to most Jews, repellent. No more shocking a reversal of their most devoutly held assumptions could possibly have been imagined. Not merely blasphemy, it was madness.[8]

It wasn't so difficult to believe some first century itinerant Jewish preacher with Messianic pretensions was put to death on a cross. Anyone perceived as a threat to the Roman state was a candidate for a cross, and the Romans were prolific practitioners of dispensing with those they deemed threats to their power. To crush especially tough rebellions and send a clear message, the Romans were known to crucify thousands of criminals along the roads like so many telephone poles lined up one after the other. Message received: Don't cross Rome or you'll end up like one of them.

What was madness to the first century Jew wasn't fellow Jews being hung on Roman crosses, but one who claimed to be the Messiah. First, there was nothing in Jewish literature that would lead anyone to think such a thing. Vermes, not a Christian, says that "neither the suffering of a Messiah, nor his death and resurrection, appear to have been part of the faith of first century Judaism."[9] Edersheim concurs: "There is one truth which, we are reluctantly obliged to admit, scarcely any parallel in the teaching of Rabbinism: it was that of a suffering Messiah."[10] Some Christians might think the suffering servant of Isaiah 53 at least gives some clue that a crucified Messiah would at least be a possibility, but such a connection never emerged. J. Gresham Machen writes, "[T]here is not the slightest evidence that the pre-Christian Jews interpreted Isaiah 53 of the vicarious sufferings of the Messiah, or had any notion of the Messiah's vicarious death."[11]

It stretches belief beyond breaking to think from a psychological perspective a Messiah on a cross would occur to any rational human being, specifically a Jewish one in the first century. Peter S. Williams says it well:

> What movement would make up a recent leader, executed by a Roman governor for treason, and then declare, "We're his followers"? If they wanted to commit suicide, there were simpler ways to do it.[12]

Jesus' Birth and Death

Which is why his followers were cowering in fear after the gruesome deed had been done—as John puts it, hiding in a room "for fear of the Jews." None of them wanted to be next to the cross for a man who was obviously not their hoped-for Messiah, and why this Jesus of Nazareth, in their minds, could never be the Messiah. For Jews, it simply wasn't that death on a cross was horrific and shameful, reserved only for the worst in society, but that being hung on a tree represented something religiously abhorrent. Every Jew at the time was familiar with these words from Deuteronomy 21:23:

> The body must not remain hanging from the tree overnight. You must bury the body that same day, for anyone who is hung is cursed in the sight of God. In this way, you will prevent the defilement of the land the LORD your God is giving you as your special possession.

No wonder his followers wanted to get Jesus off the cross so quickly. He was obviously cursed of God and would defile the land as well if left up overnight. Imagine the utter confusion of Jesus' disciples. How could such a thing happen to Jesus? According to Jewish law the punishment for blasphemy was stoning, which almost happened to Jesus several times. If it had, they might have at least been able to process it as reasonable: Jesus said and did some amazing things, but he went a little too far and paid the price. They would have been deeply disheartened, but at least a Jew could comprehend stoning for blasphemy. It would have fit into their understanding of the universe. Jesus would clearly have not been the Messiah, but he still could have been seen as a prophet. But a cross? Cursed of God? That would have been, in the overused word of Vizzini in *The Princess Bride*, inconceivable!

THREE DAYS IN THE TOMB

The crucifixion of Jesus of Nazareth under Pontius Pilate is one of the most well attested and accepted historical facts of the ancient world. Nobody makes the case that Jesus' followers fabricated it. Every scholar and historian, Christian or not, realizes Jews would *never* do that. The issue is, what *meaning* is attached to the crucifixion, and would a Jew make *that* up. The only thing that could make Jews attach the meaning they did to the cross was Jesus proving to his disciples he came back from the dead. A merely crucified Messiah who stayed dead would *never* have become what Christians proclaimed him to be from the very beginning. John Calvin in his commentary on Hebrews tells us what Christians proclaimed that would have been anathema to the Jews. Of the author's purpose he says:

> [It] was really to build up our faith, so that we may learn that God is made known to us in no other way than in Christ: for as to the essence of God, so immense is the brightness that it dazzles our eyes, except it shines on us in Christ. It hence follows, that we are blind as to the light of God, until in Christ it beams on us.[13]

If you had said such a thing to any of the disciples while Jesus' body lay in the tomb, they would have thought you certifiably insane. The essence of God is most definitely *not* displayed by a criminal mangled and dead hanging on a Roman cross, and soon to be rotting in a tomb.

Critics who believe the gospel narratives are primarily fiction rarely consider human psychology, but my whole argument is based on it. We can clearly see from the mental state of Jesus' disciples they were devastated by their ostensible Messiah turning out to be a fraud after all. What else could they think? When Jesus was arrested his closest disciples abandoned him and fled in fear, and that was before their Rabbi was crucified. After, they locked themselves in a room terrified they could easily be next. When reading Scripture, I like to see the characters as the real people they were, and then try to envision how they might emotionally respond to events that perplexed them. I imagine those Friday and Saturday nights were the longest and most painful of their lives, trying to piece together the Jesus they knew and lived with for three years with the Jesus now dead, a victim of Jewish conniving and

Roman justice. I often think of this picture when life gets difficult and confusing, and compare it to those nights of Jesus' disciples wrestling with the incomprehensible.

If we're to believe the critics, out of these terrified, confused, and dispirited Jews would come a new religion that would transform the entire world; and somehow, they made it all up! Given the theology, psychology, and worldview of this ragtag band of peasant Jews from Galilee there is only one thing that would make such a thing possible, and to that we turn next.

CHAPTER ELEVEN
THE RESURRECTION

Finally, we reach the biggest problem for the skeptics who claim Christianity is to one degree or another fiction. As I have previously discussed, non-Christians of the secular persuasion come to the table with a bias, already believing people don't come back from the dead. So, the resurrection of Jesus must have been a story invented by the religiously disillusioned who couldn't handle the death of their beloved Messiah. To the contrary, it is more difficult to believe the resurrection was invented than that it actually happened.

I've come to believe, over four decades as a Christian, that apologetics isn't primarily about convincing non-Christians and skeptics to become Christians. Rather, I see its purpose as primarily about strengthening the faith of the people of God; that is what it has meant for me. The improbability of the resurrection being made up therefore can't help but strengthen our faith. When I doubt my own resurrection, I go back to Jesus' resurrection and convince myself all over again it is true (and this book is primarily an argument to myself more than anyone else). After Jesus told Martha in John 11 that her brother Lazarus would rise again, he said to her:

> "I am the resurrection and the life. He who believes in me will live, even though he dies; [26] and whoever lives and believes in me will never die. Do you believe this?"

What kind of person says such things? Certainly not a Jesus who is the great moral teacher critics for several hundred years have insisted he is.

A merely human Jesus who said such things would be a megalomaniacal psycho case who belongs in a white jacket in a round room. Christians let critics off the hook by not forcing them into only one of two conclusions about Jesus. In the old trilemma, he was either what John reports here, or a lunatic, or a liar. C.S. Lewis put it well, "One must keep on pointing out that Christianity is a statement which, if false, is of no importance, and if true, of infinite importance. The one thing it cannot be is moderately important."[1] Our response to the resurrection should mirror Lewis. If Jesus did not rise from the dead, it is of no importance; and if he did, it is of infinite importance. One thing it cannot possibly be is moderately important. When the risen Jesus appeared to Doubting Thomas he said, "Put your finger here; see my hands. Reach out your hand and put it into my side. Stop doubting and believe." Our response should be the same as Thomas: "My Lord and my God!"

THE MYTH OF THE DYING AND RISING GOD

Doubting Thomas had good reason for doubt: Dead people don't come back to life. Those who refuse to believe in the resurrection often seek to explain it away by claiming it is another among the many myths in the ancient world of dying and rising gods. This claim is nothing new. J. Gresham Machen, fighting this back in 1921, wrote, "A tendency is found in certain recent writers to exaggerate enormously the prevalence and clarity of the pagan ideas about a dying and rising god."[2] He then goes into great detail to prove his point of how enormously exaggerated these ideas are in having any similarity or connection to the resurrection, and I might add, in a Jewish context. Yet, this is a myth that will not die, and skeptics continue to use it as if it had any legitimacy.

They generally don't assert their argument in any detail when making their claim. Rather, skeptics assume without evidence that dying and rising god myths were so prevalent in the ancient pagan world, that inevitably the same idea was planted in the minds of Jews of the time. Thus, after Jesus died it was a piece of cake for his followers to make up the story of a dying and rising Jesus. We'll see why this is ridiculous to ascribe to ancient Jews, but there is nothing even closely analogous to the gospel stories in any ancient pagan religion. Machen makes the case, exhaustively, that any influence paganism had on Judaism was superficial, if it had any influence at all.

WHAT ABOUT THAT EMPTY TOMB?

The empty tomb is something the first Christians did not have to make up. Almost all scholars agree that after the crucifixion the tomb was found empty. That's a real problem for those who insist that a dead man can't come back to life. So, it *must* be explained in some way. Ironically, the first evidence for the fact of the empty tomb came from Jesus' enemies, as we read in Matthew 28:

> [12] When the chief priests had met with the elders and devised a plan, they gave the soldiers a large sum of money, [13] telling them, "You are to say, 'His disciples came during the night and stole him away while we were asleep.' [14] If this report gets to the governor, we will satisfy him and keep you out of trouble." [15] So the soldiers took the money and did as they were instructed. And this story has been widely circulated among the Jews to this very day.

To stop this train dead in its tracks, all these Jewish leaders needed to do was to show everyone that the tomb was in fact not empty. As William Lane Craig notes, "It would have been virtually impossible for the disciples to proclaim the resurrection in Jerusalem had the tomb *not* been empty."[3] If you're going to make up an empty tomb, you don't do that in Jerusalem, because it would have been easy to prove the tomb was not empty. It's also not a good idea to do what the Apostles did from the very beginning, proclaim a risen Jesus in Jerusalem. As Peter declared in the first Christian sermon (Acts 2), "God has raised this Jesus to life, and we are all witnesses of it." Produce the body, end of story.

Not only that, but to claim the empty tomb was made up, you would have to believe that pretty much everything was, including Joseph of Arimathea and his tomb, the burial process of preparing Jesus for the tomb, the soldiers guarding it, everything. What kind of credibility would such tall tales have had in spreading the message of a new religion? Speaking of Joseph, Craig adds that, "Even the most skeptical scholars agree that it is unlikely that the figure of Joseph, as a member of the Sanhedrin could have been a Christian invention," especially since Mark tells us "that the whole Sanhedrin voted for Jesus' condemnation."[4] Why would they make up a story about a wealthy "member of the council," as John says, being a hero of the story? I don't think they would. And a new tomb for a rich family at the time was something of a status symbol; most people would likely have known the location of Joseph's tomb.

As I mentioned in a previous chapter, Jesus was way too popular to make it all up. It wasn't long after the resurrection that Jesus' disciples proclaimed him alive again, and in Jerusalem! If it were all a fairy tale it could easily be disproved, and nobody would believe it. Not to mention that a tomb with Jesus still in it may have even become a shrine of sorts, yet that never happened because the tomb was in fact empty. If there was no empty tomb there would be no Christianity. Critics will admit the empty tomb was a necessary precondition for the early and explosive growth of Christianity, but they also think it was a sufficient precondition. It was not. Without an actual resurrection there is no Christianity.

HOW DID AN EMPTY TOMB TURN INTO CHRISTIANITY?

All scholars with an anti-supernaturalist bias admit something dramatically profound *had* to happen to account for the rise of something as unlikely as early Christianity. They just *know* that an actual physical resurrection of Jesus was not it! What they refuse to admit, though, is there is just as much historical evidence for the resurrection as there is for the empty tomb. Their presuppositions make them blind to that evidence. Tim Keller puts their dilemma this way:

> Most people think that when it comes to Jesus' resurrection, the burden of proof is on believers to give evidence that it happened. That is not completely the case. The resurrection also puts a burden of proof on its non-believers. It is not enough to simply believe that Jesus did not rise from the dead. You must then come up with a historically feasible alternate explanation for the birth of the church. You have to provide some other plausible account for how things began.[5]

Finding "some other plausible" explanation is a huge problem for the skeptics, though most blow it off like the flick of a cigarette ash. Anyone who cares about the truth will take the historical evidence for the resurrection seriously. Whether or not they accept the resurrection as historical fact, they will certainly admit this is a dilemma for those whose worldview will not allow them to entertain the idea of an actual resurrection. Why is it a dilemma? Because the alternative explanations Keller refers to are weak and completely implausible. It takes far more faith to believe in any of the alternative explanations. The resurrection is the only thing that can plausibly explain the rise of Christianity against all odds, and its world transforming impact.

THE JEWS AND RESURRECTION

Before we get to the alternatives, we must consider how plausible the argument is that Jesus' disciples could make up a resurrection. First, let's deal with Jewish expectations about the concept of a resurrection. It is well known that Jews expected a general resurrection of the dead at the end of time. The idea of an individual coming back from the dead in a resurrected material body in the middle of history was completely unknown. It was also inconceivable; it would never have occurred to them that such a thing could happen, so how believable is it that they could make up such a thing?

Not only would this have been unlikely seeing the idea is never mentioned in Jewish history or teaching, but it is also never mentioned because it would have been a contradiction to everything they believed about the world and ultimate salvation from sin. The resurrection for Jews was solely an eschatological concept, something that will happen at the end of time when all sin, suffering, and death is dealt with once and for all. One person rising from the dead in the middle of history with a continuation of fallen reality was incompatible with everything they believed about resurrection. If they were to make up the resurrection of Jesus, they would have to invent a concept nobody had ever thought of in the 1,500-year history of the Jewish religion.

DID THEY STEAL THE BODY?

Setting aside the improbability of Jews making up the resurrection of Jesus, neither were Jesus' disciples in any shape emotionally or psychologically to have done so. Their confusion and distress by events that happened so quickly, compounded by mourning the death of the man they thought their beloved Messiah, makes them unlikely candidates as masterminds of a conspiracy to deceive the Roman government of Judea and the Jewish leaders of Jerusalem. Not only that, but they would also have been deceiving Jesus' followers, and then have openly lied about it for the rest of their lives, even as they gave their lives for what they knew to be a lie. Eighteenth century Christian philosopher William Paley asks this question:

> Would men in such circumstances pretend to have seen what they never saw; assert facts which they had no knowledge of, go about lying to teach virtue; and, though not only convinced of Christ being an imposter, but having seen the success of his imposture in his crucifixion, yet persist in carrying on; and so persist, as to bring upon themselves, for nothing, and with full knowledge of the consequences, enmity and hatred, danger and death?[6]

The question answers itself.

OTHER OPTIONS?

If Jesus didn't come back from the dead, as the witnesses boldly proclaim from the beginning to the end of their lives, there are only two other equally implausible options than his disciples stealing the body. One is that he didn't really die on the cross, known as "the swoon theory;" and the other is that somehow the body disappeared, and his followers thought they experienced a risen Jesus. We don't have to deal with these in any detail because neither passes "the smell test." For the former, if Jesus somehow survived something the Romans were particularly good at, and had extensive experience doing, Jesus wouldn't have been in good shape. An ER with modern medicine would have had a hard time keeping him alive. He certainly wouldn't have been the Jesus they boldly proclaimed as risen, a victor over sin and death, one to be worshiped as Thomas said as Lord and God.

The only other option to an actual physical resurrection, stolen body, or swoon theory, is that the tomb was in fact empty, and Jesus' disciples *thought* they saw Jesus. These appearances of Jesus, while not real, had the effect as if they were real, and boom—Christianity exploded! German higher critics of the 19th century, and liberal Christians of the early 20th, were fond of arguing for this spiritual Jesus somehow appearing, and the disciples having what they called a "resurrection experience." The historicity of the event was beside the point; and we all "know" people don't come back from the dead, especially after the Romans got done with them. Jesus' followers were so distraught, the argument goes, and so longing for the crucified Messiah to come back to them somehow, that their minds conjured up a Jesus who came back from the dead. Then, because of this "spiritual" experience, they went throughout the Roman Empire proclaiming a resurrected Lord. The problem with this explanation is however it was explained—by dreams, visions, or mass hallucinations—it all comes up against the same cold hard truth: For Jews, a resurrection of one man in the middle of history was inconceivable, as was a resurrection not bodily and physical. We ought to carefully consider if they could make up, imagine, or dream of something they could not conceive.

WHAT DOES THE NEW TESTAMENT ACTUALLY SAY ABOUT THE RESURRECTION?

All the alternative explanations either ignore or discount the actual New Testament witness to the resurrection by, as we've learned, begging the question. Even just positing God as a possibility makes the resurrection possible, and thus allows us to judge the historical and textual evidence more accurately. It is extremely compelling evidence. Given the theme of the book, I'm not going to offer a typical apologetic defense of the resurrection. There are many wonderful resources available from scholars such as Gary Habermas, Mike Licona and others; they and other scholars make the uninvented argument to great effect.

WHY ARE THERE NO DEPICTIONS OF THE RESURRECTION?

First, isn't it curious that the gospels don't say anything about the actual resurrection of Jesus? Why would that be? Probably because there were no direct eyewitnesses. As I've said, nobody expected Jesus to come back to life, so like fans at a rock concert they didn't camp out at the tomb on the night before the third day dawned to catch the big event. Let's say Jews *could* make up a resurrection in the middle of history. Human nature being what it is, would they not describe the resurrection in *some* way? Tell us how it happened—You know, big earthquake, shining light, angels, Jesus appearing in bright lights, etc.? Geisler and Turk explain, "Embellished and extravagant details are strong signs that a historical account has legendary elements." Then they provide a long quote from something known as the *Gospel of Peter* written over 100 years after Jesus, which was definitely not written by Peter.[7] It is very impressive *if* you're making up a story of a resurrection. Legends and fairy tales, made up stuff, as the critics insist the resurrection is, are all about embellished and extravagant details. The gospel accounts, on the contrary, are stark and simple; and we only infer that a resurrection happened by an empty tomb and eyewitness testimony of those who claimed they saw Jesus alive again. What we read in the gospels is believable if it's true, but not at all if it's made up.

THE CRITERION OF EMBARRASSMENT

Second, if all we have are inferences and eyewitness testimony, does any of it appear that it could be made up? Let's start with the criterion of embarrassment, or if you're making up a story, you don't make up stuff that makes you look bad. We're now at the point where we are reasonably convinced Jesus of Nazareth died on a Roman cross and was buried in a tomb which was discovered to be empty three days later. Now what? We read these astonishing words from Luke 24:

> On the first day of the week, very early in the morning, the women took the spices they had prepared and went to the tomb. [2] They found the stone rolled away from the tomb, [3] but when they entered, they did not find the body of the Lord Jesus.

Not only are women the first to find the tomb empty, but we also read in Matthew they were the first to see the resurrected Jesus:

> [8] So the women hurried away from the tomb, afraid yet filled with joy, and ran to tell his disciples. [9] Suddenly Jesus met them. "Greetings," he said. They came to him, clasped his feet and worshiped him. [10] Then Jesus said to them, "Do not be afraid. Go and tell my brothers to go to Galilee; there they will see me."

Why are these accounts astonishing? Women! Looking back 20 centuries from the present day, nobody bats an eye and asks, why *not* women? There are two reasons, which are both embarrassing to the nascent Christian movement. First, the testimony of women as the first eyewitnesses is a big problem for the skeptics. Craig Keener gives us the scholarly consensus on this issue:

> The witness of women at the tomb is very likely historical, precisely because it was so offensive to the larger culture—not the sort of testimony one would invent... [M]ost of Jesus' Jewish contemporaries held much less esteem for the testimony of women than for that of men; this suspicion reflects a broader Mediterranean limited trust of women's speech and testimony enshrined in Roman law.[8]

If you want people to believe your story in the first century, you *don't* make women the first witnesses. Not only this, but the men don't exactly come off looking like pillars of the early church; they look more like cowards. After they ran away from Jesus in his hour of need, and Peter denied three times even knowing him,[9] they ended up cowering in a locked room because they didn't want to be next. Then, when the women told them they saw the risen Jesus, how did they respond? Pretty much like any men of their time would, but certainly not like disciples of Jesus should (Luke 24):

> [9] When they came back from the tomb, they told all these things to the Eleven and to all the others. [10] It was Mary Magdalene, Joanna, Mary the mother of James, and the others with them who told this to the apostles. [11] But they did not believe the women, because their words seemed to them like nonsense.

The Greek word used by Luke reflects the male bias against women at the time. They thought it was silly or idle talk, folly. As Thomas says in *Jesus of Nazareth*, "Women's fantasies." So not only do the gospel authors make the women look good, but they also make the men look bad. Is this how men in a male dominated culture would invent a story if they wanted other men to believe it? Doubtful. It's much easier to believe the authors were communicating historical events pretty much as they happened, embarrassing or not.

One more embarrassing story, and then we'll see exactly what the early Christians declared about this Jesus they proclaimed had risen from

The Resurrection

the dead. Christians around the world are familiar with what happened on the road to Emmaus on that first Easter Sunday (Luke 24). Jesus walks up to two disciples on the road like he's one of the multitudes of visitors to Jerusalem for the Passover, and he asks them what they're talking about. They're surprised because everybody is talking about Jesus of Nazareth. They tell him what happened, including the empty tomb and news from angels that Jesus was alive. His response is priceless, and speaks to the utter cluelessness of all the disciples:

> [25] He said to them, "How foolish you are, and how slow to believe all that the prophets have spoken! [26] Did not the Messiah have to suffer these things and then enter his glory?" [27] And beginning with Moses and all the Prophets, he explained to them what was said in all the Scriptures concerning himself.

I love the Greek word Luke uses for foolish: non-thinking, i.e., not "reasoning through" a matter (with proper logic); unmindful, which describes acting in a "mindless, dense" way ("just plain stupid"). That pretty much describes everybody who encounters Jesus, before *and* after the resurrection. When they get to the village, the two disciples urge Jesus to stay with them. Right before they are going to eat dinner Jesus reveals himself to them; and when they recognize it's him, he disappears. They instantly head back to Jerusalem to tell everyone it is true; Jesus has risen! What happens next adds to the embarrassment:

> [36] While they were still talking about this, Jesus himself stood among them and said to them, "Peace be with you."

> [37] They were startled and frightened, thinking they saw a ghost. [38] He said to them, "Why are you troubled, and why do doubts rise in your minds? [39] Look at my hands and my feet. It is I myself! Touch me and see; a ghost does not have flesh and bones, as you see I have."

Many of the disciples witnessed, and they all knew, that Jesus had been beaten, nailed to a cross, died, and was buried. Even after the women told them, they didn't believe it; and now, here is Jesus himself, and they still don't believe it! He is even willing to condescend to their cluelessness (as God always does with us) by proving it to them. He even chows down some food while they are watching so there can be no doubt. He is Jesus of Nazareth, alive! It's hard to imagine them having made up this story, and all under the rubric, "How could you be so stupid!"

THE EFFECT OF THE RESURRECTION

As I said previously, something must explain the rise of Christianity as a world transforming religion. All scholars, regardless of their views on the historicity of the gospels, agree that Jesus' followers *believed* they saw him risen from the dead. The nature of the resurrection they proclaimed all throughout that first generation of Christians is reflected in the Luke 24 passage; Jesus has a real, material physical body. In John 21, in what John says is Jesus' third appearance to them, Jesus meets the disciples by the Sea of Galilee. He helps them to a miraculously large catch of fish, and then invites them to have breakfast with him. To the first Christians, Jesus was no apparition, no ghost as they initially thought. Read through Acts, and it is obvious the Apostles proclaimed a physical, bodily resurrection of Jesus from the very beginning. (See Peter's sermon in Acts 2, and the other sermons and speeches in Acts.) The Apostle Paul, who came to the table a little late, makes these astonishing assertions in I Corinthians 15:

> [3] For what I received I passed on to you as of first importance: that Christ died for our sins according to the Scriptures, [4] that he was buried, that he was raised on the third day according to the Scriptures, [5] and that he appeared to Cephas, and then to the Twelve. [6] After that, he appeared to more than five hundred of the brothers at the same time, most of whom are still living, though some have fallen asleep. [7] Then he appeared to James, then to

all the apostles, [8] and last of all he appeared to me also, as to one abnormally born.

Scholars agree Paul's reference to what he received came from the Apostles when he visited Jerusalem three years after his conversion. They were not proclaiming a religious "experience," but the God-man come back to life. Mere religious experiences don't have the power to do what happened to those first Jewish followers of Jesus. The immediate, drastic changes in their religious convictions can only be explained by the resurrection, and Jesus proving it beyond a shadow of a doubt. Even if these Jews could have somehow made-up something inconceivable to them, or be deluded into believing it, none of that could explain the emergence of a new religion out of their Judaism, nor its explosive growth. J.P. Moreland says anyone "who denies the resurrection owes us an explanation of this transformation which does justice to the historical facts." Skeptics don't like these historical facts because, well, resurrections can't happen! Let's confuse them with these facts they have no ability to explain apart from the supernatural. According to Moreland, the first Christians, strict Jews all, immediately gave up these Jewish convictions that defined everything about their religion:

1. The sacrificial system.
2. The importance of keeping the law.
3. Keeping of the Sabbath.
4. Non-Trinitarian theism.
5. A human Messiah.[10]

The skeptic says, "Yeah, so what. No big deal; it happens every day of the week." Well, if it does, I'm waiting for concrete evidence. Instead, we generally get anti-supernatural bias disguised as above-it-all, supposedly-objective assertions with little basis in historical fact. As Moreland says in a bit of understatement, "The resurrection offers the only rational explanation."[11]

For our final excursion into our Uninvented Bible, we'll take a brief look at the Apostle Paul who is an especially difficult one for the skeptics to explain away. The resurrection is the only realistic explanation for him too!

CHAPTER TWELVE
THE APOSTLE PAUL

It can be argued that the Apostle Paul is the most influential figure in all human history (without Paul no one may have ever heard of Jesus). While some radical skeptics don't believe Jesus even existed, nobody, not one historian or scholar I know of, would ever claim Paul did not exist. For an ancient, Paul was a voluminous writer, and ancient writers are much harder to dismiss. What we find in our New Testament is probably a small portion of his actual letters. The issue isn't whether the Apostle Paul existed, but most troubling for the skeptic is, how did *Saul* become Paul? Paul's conversion is especially difficult for the skeptic to explain away. I once heard someone say how unlikely his conversion would have been. Not unlikely as in, wow, that's surprising, but… that just can't be! He gave a couple examples of equally unlikely conversions. Imagine Winston Churchill becoming a Marxist. Or Hitler becoming a Jew. The Hebrew Pharisee Saul becoming the Christian Apostle Paul is every bit as unimaginable.

Paul's conversion is the primary event in his life skeptics must explain away, and the reason brings us back to a phrase I hope you remember when you finish reading this book: *question begging anti-supernatural bias*. Certainly, Jesus couldn't have appeared to Paul on the road to Damascus because, well, Jesus was dead, and dead people don't come back to life. Therefore, Jesus couldn't appear to Saul, as he was then named. See how this works? But the radical conversion of Paul is one of the most well-attested facts of the ancient world; and nobody denies it, so it must be explained somehow. Only for the skeptic, the supernatural elements need to be explained away. I haven't done any in-depth study of those who engage in such anti-supernatural arguments for Paul's conversion, but I'm confident they'd be even less persuasive than the anti-supernatural arguments for the empty tomb and the subsequent growth of the church. The only real option is psychological (Paul *thought* he saw the risen Jesus), and then engage in some Freudian or Jungian analysis of his upbringing and mental state, and pile conjecture upon conjecture. Or maybe they should just believe Paul's own testimony (Gal. 1):

> [11] I want you to know, brothers and sisters, that the gospel I preached is not of human origin. [12] I did not receive it from any man, nor was I taught it; rather, I received it by revelation from Jesus Christ.
>
> [13] For you have heard of my previous way of life in Judaism, how intensely I persecuted the church of God and tried to destroy it. [14] I was advancing in Judaism beyond many of my own age among my people and was extremely zealous for the traditions of my fathers. [15] But when God, who set me apart from my mother's womb and called me by his grace, was pleased [16] to reveal his Son in me so that I might preach him among the Gentiles, my immediate response was not to consult any human being. [17] I did not go up to Jerusalem to see those who were apostles before I was, but I went into Arabia. Later I returned to Damascus.
>
> [18] Then after three years, I went up to Jerusalem to get acquainted with Cephas and stayed with him fifteen days. [19] I saw none of the other apostles—only James, the Lord's brother. [20] I assure you before God that what I am writing you is no lie.

Galatians is one of the "undisputed" letters of Paul, meaning scholars of even the most skeptical stripe are convinced that Paul wrote it. Thus, we have a choice: either what Paul says here is true, and we believe his assurance, or he is lying. Anti-supernaturalists, though, insist there is a third option. While Paul obviously didn't see Jesus on that road, he wasn't in fact lying because he *thinks* he is telling the truth. That whole "road to Damascus" experience only happened in his head, maybe with some natural explanation for bright lights and such; but Paul really, really thought he saw Jesus, thus he wasn't lying.

The problem with this anti-supernaturalist reading is the historical record. The only reason we know this happened on a road to Damascus is because Luke records the event in Acts 9; and as a companion of Paul on his missionary journeys, Luke likely got the story from the horse's mouth, so to speak. We know he was a close brother and friend of Paul because they spent a lot of time together, as we learn from what are called the "we passages" in Acts where Luke moves from describing events in the third person, to the first person. For example, in Acts 16:10-17 Luke writes, "After Paul had seen the vision, we got ready at once to leave for Macedonia, concluding that God had called us to preach the gospel to them." The other "we passages" are in Acts 20:5-15, Acts 21:1-18, and Acts 27:1-28:16. Paul also says of Luke in his letters that he was "the beloved physician" (Col. 4:14). He tells Timothy when he was in Rome, "Only Luke is with me" (1 Tim. 4:11). He also calls Luke one of his "fellow workers" (Phil. 1:24). Luke knew Paul as well as anyone, and there is nothing about what happened on the road to Damascus to suggest it was merely a psychological event in Paul's brain. Here is how Luke describes what proved to be the greatest inflection point in human history (Acts 9):

> Meanwhile, Saul was still breathing out murderous threats against the Lord's disciples. He went to the high priest [2] and asked him for letters to the synagogues in Damascus, so that if he found any there who belonged to the Way, whether men or women, he might take them as prisoners to Jerusalem. [3] As he neared Damascus on his journey,

suddenly a light from heaven flashed around him. ⁴ He fell to the ground and heard a voice say to him, "Saul, Saul, why do you persecute me?"

⁵ "Who are you, Lord?" Saul asked.

"I am Jesus, whom you are persecuting," he replied. ⁶ "Now get up and go into the city, and you will be told what you must do."

⁷ The men traveling with Saul stood there speechless; they heard the sound but did not see anyone. ⁸ Saul got up from the ground, but when he opened his eyes he could see nothing. So they led him by the hand into Damascus. ⁹ For three days he was blind, and did not eat or drink anything.

We'll discuss the Saul of "murderous threats" below, but we're again confronted with the persistent issue any Bible reader must honestly address: Is this historical? Did it happen, or not? As we've seen, the writers of the gospels, including Luke, were clearly attempting to write history. If we can get beyond our tendency to anti-supernatural bias (and it affects all of us to one degree or another, Christians or not), we are free to assess the evidence of the text itself, and not read our prejudice into it. With bias, we have to conclude it's made up; without, we can take seriously what is presented in the text as straightforward history of a supernatural event. It was also not Paul alone having the experience, but several others who witnessed it. Something happened, and it happened instantly. In Damascus not long after, the Lord appeared to a man named Ananias and told him to go and lay his hands on Saul to restore his sight. Ananias' reply reflects the Saul everyone knew about, and the one they were expecting:

¹³ "Lord," Ananias answered, "I have heard many reports about this man and all the harm he has done to your holy people in Jerusalem. ¹⁴ And he has come here with

authority from the chief priests to arrest all who call on your name."

After being rebuked by the Lord for questioning him, Ananias goes to see Saul, and his sight is restored. It is difficult to explain what happened next unless it really happened:

> Saul spent several days with the disciples in Damascus. [20] At once he began to preach in the synagogues that Jesus is the Son of God. [21] All those who heard him were astonished and asked, "Isn't he the man who raised havoc in Jerusalem among those who call on this name? And hasn't he come here to take them as prisoners to the chief priests?" [22] Yet Saul grew more and more powerful and baffled the Jews living in Damascus by proving that Jesus is the Messiah.

It would be like being in a worship service at a Jewish synagogue in Nazi Germany in the mid-1930s and seeing Adolf Hitler come waltzing in wearing a prayer shawl and yarmulke. There would be a lot of cases of severe whiplash. To see and hear Paul preaching about Jesus as the Messiah mere days after getting to Damascus was every bit as shocking as Hitler embracing Judaism. A mere hallucination can't explain it. And nobody could make it up because it was Paul's declaration of his conversion for the rest of his life. How best to explain it? God!

A HEBREW OF HEBREWS

As for the "murderous threats," the conversion of Saul is most plausibly explained by it happening exactly as Luke describes it. The reason is found in why he was so rabidly anti-Christian. Saul's parents obviously had big plans for the young man, and he was sent from his hometown of Tarsus to Jerusalem to study under one of the great Rabbis of the day, Gamaliel. Known as something of a moderate, his pupil Saul most certainly would not be. Steeped in Judaism, it defined everything about him. In his own words (Phil. 3):

> If someone else thinks they have reasons to put confidence in the flesh, I have more: [5] circumcised on the eighth day, of the people of Israel, of the tribe of Benjamin, a Hebrew of Hebrews; in regard to the law, a Pharisee; [6] as for zeal, persecuting the church; as for righteousness based on the law, faultless.

The first king of Israel came from the tribe of Benjamin, and was Paul's namesake, Saul. After Paul was arrested, and before appealing to Caesar, he was sent to Rome and spoke to the people in Aramaic confirming his zeal for Judaism prior to his conversion (Acts 22):

> [3] "I am a Jew, born in Tarsus of Cilicia, but brought up in this city. I studied under Gamaliel and was thoroughly trained in the law of our ancestors. I was just as zealous for God as any of you are today. [4] I persecuted the followers of this Way to their death, arresting both men and women and throwing them into prison, [5] as the high priest and all the Council can themselves testify. I even obtained letters from them to their associates in Damascus, and went there to bring these people as prisoners to Jerusalem to be punished.

He then goes into detail about his conversion experience and encounter with Jesus of Nazareth. I imagine Paul recounted his coming face to face with the risen Jesus many times during his life, and every time he believed it was real. The only plausible explanation for his life and influence on world history is that his encounter with Jesus was indeed real, not a figment of his imagination.

PAUL'S MISSION TO THE GENTILES

What is every bit as radical and unexpected as Paul's conversion was his teaching and missionary obsession. The reason for the latter was the former. Until Paul, religion had never been considered universal in scope. The Jews should have known better because God's promise to Abraham was that through him, and thus Israel, all the nations of the earth would be blessed (Gen. 12). The Lord gave them an important hint through Isaiah (42:6, 49:6) when He said Israel would be "a light to the Gentiles." By the time of Jesus, however, Jews wouldn't even eat with Gentiles, let alone be a light and blessing to them. For the pagans it was the same but for quite different reasons. Martin Goodman explains:

> The sense of mission set Christians apart from other religious groups, including Jews, in the early Roman empire. The notion that it is desirable for existing enthusiasts to encourage outsiders to worship the god to whom they are devoted was not obvious in the ancient world… On the contrary, it was common for pagans to take pride in the local nature of their religious lives, establishing a special relationship between themselves and the god of a family or place, without wishing, let alone expecting, others to join in worshiping the same god. Christians in the first generation were different, espousing a proselytizing mission which was a shocking novelty in the ancient world. Only familiarity makes us fail to appreciate the extraordinary ambition of Paul, who seems to have invented the notion of a systematic conversion of the whole world, area by geographical area.[1]

Although he qualifies it with "seems to," we're to believe Paul "invented" this notion of converting the entire world all by himself. We would have to believe he made it up because of some non-supernatural "experience" he had as he was going to persecute the followers of "the Way?" Then he immediately starts proclaiming the message of those he was supposed to be persecuting? Not only that, but in doing so he goes against every cultural instinct of literally every single person in the world, Jew and pagan alike, including fellow followers of "the Way?" Somehow, in due course he comes up with the notion out of nowhere that every person in the world needs to be converted and believe this? I would maintain a more believable and plausible explanation is God!

The God-ordained nature of Paul's mission becomes even more apparent when we understand the dynamic of the early Jewish church, and the intense struggle he had moving outside the bounds of Judaism. We see this played out in Acts and described by Paul in his epistles as he confronts the Judaizers. It's difficult to imagine what would motivate Paul to invent an idea so against the religious expectations of the entire world without divine intervention. There are numerous examples we can cite. Peter the great pillar and leader of the early church is an illuminating one. If it were not for God revealing the truth to Peter in a vision, and Paul confronting his hypocrisy in the face of the Jewish temptation to treat Gentiles as strangers to God's covenant, Christianity would likely never have become the world transforming religion it became. It's difficult to believe this whole dynamic, and the struggle inherent in it, was an invention by the early Christian community, or Paul himself. It reads like history.

First to Peter's vision. In Acts 10 Peter is confronted with his culturally determined Jewish bias against Gentiles as "unclean," and his response to God's revelation is telling; he's shocked to learn the truth. As the story goes, Cornelius, a God-fearing Roman centurion, is given a vision of an angel of God who tells him to have Peter brought to him. At the same time, Peter is having his own vision with the message from God, "Do not call anything impure that God has made clean." As he's wondering what this all means, men arrive and tell him about Cornelius' vision, and that Peter is to go with them to meet the centurion. As you read through the story it reads so powerfully real. You'll remember we call that verisimilitude, and it's all over the Bible. We must ask, given the dynamics of the time, who would invent the unimaginable idea, to Jews, of a Jew breaking down the seemingly impenetrable wall of separation between Jew and Gentile? Without the vision, Peter would never have thought that such a thing was even possible, let alone a God-ordained goal. Yet, even with the vision, Peter succumbed to the continued tendency to Jewish isolation.

The Apostle Paul

In Galatians 2 we read about Paul calling out Peter's hypocrisy. It is a scene unlikely to have been invented because it makes Peter, the leader of the early church, look so bad. We referred to that earlier as the criterion of embarrassment. Where would Paul get the, let's call it hutzpah, to confront Peter, the great apostle, to his face in front of so many people? Not to mention confronting him in Antioch, one of the great centers of the early church where everyone would have heard about it; natural explanations for Paul's motivation to do this are not persuasive. I'll let Paul explain the shocking episode:

> [12] Before certain men came from James, [Peter] used to eat with the Gentiles. But when they arrived, he began to draw back and separate himself from the Gentiles because he was afraid of those who belonged to the circumcision group. [13] The other Jews joined him in his hypocrisy, so that by their hypocrisy even Barnabas was led astray.
>
> [14] When I saw that they were not acting in line with the truth of the gospel, I said to Cephas in front of them all, "You are a Jew, yet you live like a Gentile and not like a Jew. How is it, then, that you force Gentiles to follow Jewish customs?"

Ouch! Remember, Paul was the *only* one in all Jewish Christianity, including its leaders, to affirm full Gentile inclusion in the church.

There are plenty of other examples of why it was so difficult for Paul to take the gospel beyond Judaism. During his missionary journeys when they entered a town, he and his companions would always start preaching at the synagogues first. As he stated in Romans 1:16, "I am not ashamed of the gospel, because it is the power of God that brings salvation to everyone who believes: first to the Jew, then to the Gentile." Many times, the Jews did not take kindly to Paul telling the Jews since they rejected his message, he was going to take it to the Gentiles. Another issue that made it difficult was many early Jewish Christians believed circumcision was still a requirement for the life of

God's people which was finally addressed at the council of Jerusalem (Acts 15) around 50 AD. Even with Peter's vision that council wouldn't have happened without Paul and his teaching, and Christianity would never have become the religion of the Gentiles that it became. One man stood against the grain, going against the overwhelming tide of all cultural expectation to break down the wall of separation between Jew and Gentile, and what do we get from Martin Goodman and others like him? Oh, Paul probably invented it. Not likely.

On the Pagan side of the equation, what Paul was doing was equally as disturbing to them as it was to the Jews. Syncretism was the religion of the ancient pagan world, and to require someone to give up every allegiance for just one God or one religion was unheard of at the time, and deeply unpopular. Even though Jews rejected such Syncretism, they never had a vision or mission to turn all pagans into Jews. Christianity for Paul was world conquering or nothing, and Paul doesn't invent that all by himself.

PAUL'S WORLD TRANSFORMING TEACHING

I will briefly address two broad areas of Paul's teaching that radically contrast with his Jewish upbringing and Jewish teaching of the time. To people like Martin Goodman, Paul's teaching like his missionary obsession was an invention. This is another example of how bias would compel someone to no other conclusion. Without bias, though, the more plausible explanation for Paul's teaching is that Jesus himself revealed it to him. As a Jew of his time, a devout and educated Pharisaical Jew no less, Paul could never have conceived what would become the Pauline theology of Romans, Galatians, Ephesians, etc.

Scholars and historians are certainly right that without Paul, Jesus' teaching, and his life, death, and resurrection would never have had the world transforming power it proved to have. As we have seen, it most likely would have remained within the narrow confines of Judaism never to have been the blessing it has proved to be for 2,000 years to every nation, tribe, and people in every language. In the 19th and early 20th centuries, critics on the other hand developed the idea that the Christianity of Paul was different from the Christianity of Jesus, as in the former was not derived from the latter. They claim Paul invented it. In 1921 J. Gresham Machen said, "The current reconstruction of Christianity had produced a Jesus and a Paul who really had little in common with each other."[2] At the same time, what Machen says elsewhere is also true, "The establishment of Christianity as a world religion, to almost as great an extent as any great historical movement can be ascribed to one man, was the work of Paul."[3] It wasn't, though, that Paul's teaching was different from the Jesus of the gospels, as the critics contend. Rather the significance of Jesus wasn't his teaching per se, but the accomplishment of his redemptive purposes, and the implication of that for his people. This is significant because everyone who rejects Paul's teaching turns the full meaning of Jesus' life into mere moralism. Machen explains:

> The religion of Paul is a religion of redemption. Jesus, according to Paul, came to earth not to say something, but to do something; He was primarily not a teacher, but a Redeemer. He came, not to teach men how to live, but to give them a new life through his atoning death. He was, indeed, also a teacher, and Paul attended to his teaching. But his teaching was all in vain unless it led to the final acceptance of his redemptive work. Not the details of Jesus' life, therefore, but the redemptive acts of death and resurrection are at the center of the religion of Paul. The teaching and example of Jesus, according to Paul, are valuable only as a means to an end.[4]

The Messiah of Jewish expectation was not a sin-bearing redeemer who would be punished for the sins of his people. There is not even a trace of such an idea in pre-Christian Jewish literature.[5] Of the idea of original sin Edersheim says, "The statement that as in Adam all spiritually died, so in Messiah all should be made alive, finds absolutely no parallel in Jewish writings."[6] Where, then, would Paul have come up with such an idea if not in the Judaism he was raised and immersed in? It is not there. Machen points out, "[T]here is not the slightest evidence that the pre-Christian Jews interpreted Isaiah 53 of the vicarious sufferings of the Messiah or had any notion of a Messiah's vicarious death."[7] He adds, "the striking fact is that Paul agrees with Jesus in just those matters to which Judaism was most singly opposed."[8]

Another area of Paul's teaching that was mind blowing and incomprehensible to Jew and Gentile alike is found throughout his letters, and can be summarized in these words from Galatians 3:28:

> There is neither Jew nor Greek, neither slave nor free, nor
> is there male and female, for you are all one in Christ Jesus.

The implications of this verse turned every cultural assumption of every person in the ancient world upside down and inside out. It would have been positively ludicrous to even say such a thing at the time, let alone believe and try to live it. Yet, there was Paul teaching it throughout the Roman empire as the logical conclusion of God redeeming his people in Christ and saving them from their sin. It was so radical that it can plausibly be argued no one at the time could have invented it on their own; and it was only that it was in fact true, and revealed, that it eventually transformed the world. As I've said many times, we take these ideas for granted because the modern world, and our values, were made possible by them. We've lived with their assumptions for almost 2,000 years, so they almost seem natural, like the way the world is supposed to be. Only it isn't! In his book *Dominion*, Tom Holland writes specifically of Paul's egalitarian teaching in Galatians:

> The malign powers that previously had kept them enslaved have been routed by Christ's victory on the cross. The fabric of things was rent, a new order of time had come into existence, and all that previously had served to separate people was now, as a consequence,

dissolved… Only the world turned upside down could ever have sanctioned such an unprecedented, such a revolutionary, announcement.[9]

Yet, we're to believe somehow Paul could have made this up all by himself? In fact, I heard an interview of Holland addressing skeptics who think Jesus didn't even exist, and he talked about how amazingly unique Christianity was in the ancient world. He said if Jesus didn't exist then Christianity is even more impressive because it took numerous people to make it all up, and then sell it as if it were *not* made-up. These made-up ideas, then, somehow completely transformed the world. As I say all the time, lies do not do that.

It is far easier to believe the Jewish people, the rock-star-and-conundrum Jesus, the miracles, his teaching, birth, death, and resurrection, the Apostle Paul, and the entire history of redemption found in our Bibles is true, than to believe it is a product of human imagination. The reader will have to judge if I've made the case.

CONCLUDING THOUGHTS

Learning more about the Bible's critics over the years, I've concluded it is the arbitrary nature of their assertions that makes their arguments so specious. The definition of specious perfectly captures why this is so pernicious: "Having the ring of truth or plausibility but actually fallacious; Deceptively appealing." It was this deceptive appeal that slowly turned Christian institutions of higher education founded in the 17th and 18th centuries into secular institutions today opposed to everything Christian.[1] This deceptive appeal eventually drove the mainline denominations into the arms of heretical liberal Christianity, resulting in their mostly empty churches. This appeal permeates the secular culture creating unnecessary doubt about the divine reliability of the Bible, even for Christians. It doesn't have to be that way.

Since the Enlightenment, Christians have increasingly been put on the defensive for their faith. Culturally, the default worldview became one of Enlightenment naturalism which in due course came to be seen as needing no defense. The supernatural claims of the Bible were treated as relics of a pre-scientific age. The enlightened of the Enlightenment "knew" better. Ironically, it was the science of Sir Isaac Newton (1642-1727), a devout Christian himself, that was the primary driver of the acceptance of naturalism as the default worldview of Western educated secular elites. Those who imbibed Newton's physics came to see the universe as a closed system of cause and effect; a cosmic machine that ran on its own without any tinkering by a creator God. The 18th century West wasn't ready to completely give up on the idea of God, so we see the growth of deism, which was reflected in the worldview of many of America's Founding Fathers. Thomas Jefferson, one of the most Deistic of the Founders, even went so far as to create his very own Bible in which he cut out all the supernatural parts. He liked the great-moral-teacher Jesus but couldn't accept anything supernatural. In this he was a forerunner of the German higher critics we discussed in the first chapter.

All these centuries of intellectual foment were part of a fascinating process of the secularization of the Christian West. Christianity went from dominant to defensive in historically short order. Many contend the "Scopes Monkey Trial" in 1925 was when Christian cultural defeat was officially declared, but that was the trickle-down effect of ideas starting centuries earlier. As philosophy increasingly became anti-God, science, technology, and material progress *seemed* to make God irrelevant. Slowly but surely the dominant drivers of cultural influence, i.e., media, education, and entertainment, became thoroughly secular. Secularism, contrary to the first amendment of the Constitution, became America's established religion, and the tyranny of secularist orthodoxy became the entrenched order by the middle of the 20th century. But something strange happened on the way to total secular domination—religion wouldn't go away. Christianity's enduring strength bewilders our cultural elites because they were certain as science and knowledge progressed, religion would wither on the vine. By the 1960s most sociologists were convinced modernization meant the end of religion; but much to their chagrin that hasn't happened, and Christianity worldwide is stronger than ever.

The historical process of secularization can be seen in parallel attacks on the two foundations of biblical religion: God's revelation in creation and in Scripture. God is revealing (pun intended) something of his sense of humor in this process. He was teasing humanity in its hubris, allowing them to think they could finally be rid of him, a la Satan's temptation to Eve; it seemed to many that man would finally "be like God knowing good and evil" (Gen. 3). But something painfully ironic happened on the way to man's deification—the 20th century. There were some minor speed bumps, like the sinking of Titanic, which because of the faith in

Concluding Thoughts

human ingenuity most people believed unsinkable. This tragedy was followed shortly by the most educated people and civilizations in the world declaring war on one another and executing meaningless carnage on a scale hitherto unimaginable. The supposed "war to end all wars" in a mere generation led to the Second World War that was even more deadly. To add insult to injury, a hundred million plus people were killed in the name of Marx's communism, and humanity's confidence in their ability to create Utopia on earth was taking a beating. Then, what has come to be called "the 60s" happened, and the ideas that had percolated among Western intelligentsia for several hundred years broke out to the wider culture like a neutron bomb.

Despite more than a century of evidence for secularism's failures, sinful human beings are stubborn, so secularism isn't going anywhere soon. However, the growth in human knowledge, scientific and otherwise, has allowed Christians to go on the offensive, in turn forcing atheists, materialists, and agnostics to go on the defensive. An increasing number of honest ones realize the burden of proof has been slowly shifting to them over the last 50 years. Regarding creation, Paul famously says in Romans 1:20, "Since the creation of the world God's invisible qualities—his eternal power and divine nature—have been clearly seen, being understood from what has been made, so they are without excuse." As I referenced in the chapter on revelation, scientific discoveries in the last 100 years are making the invisible God more clearly seen than ever before. I recently heard an interview with Eric Metaxas and Stephen C. Meyer discussing his book *The Return of the God Hypothesis*. In it he addresses three significant discoveries made in the last century that have put the materialists squarely on the defensive:

- The Big Bang
- The Fine tuning of the universe
- The discovery of digital code and information processing systems in the cell

I love a phrase Metaxas used in the conversation: It is all *preposterously complex*, yet the atheist materialists want us to believe it's all a result of random chance. There is something pathetic seeing the lengths materialists will go to deny the glaringly obvious, that the universe was created by God.

Over the same time as these scientific discoveries were happening, a similar parallel process was happening regarding God's revelation of himself in the Bible. Although not as striking and apparent to the average person as creation, it also reveals something of God's sense of humor. German higher criticism was a 19th century juggernaut aimed squarely at the credibility of Scripture. Liberal Christianity swallowed it, hook, line, and sinker; and the secular culture predictably applauded. Conservative Christians, however, adamantly refused to give up the supernatural character of the Bible, and historical, archeological, and textual scholarship in the last 50 years has made incredible strides in defending the historical reliability of the biblical text. Philosophically, Christian scholars have upped their game as well; and the intellectual environment is no longer so one-sided as it once was. The apologetics renaissance continues to make gains so Christians can stand confidently in the faith once for all delivered to the saints.

As I started thinking about writing this book, I originally thought of calling it "psychological apologetics," because I wanted to explore how biblical characters displayed what we might call psychological verisimilitude. By now, I hope I have successfully conveyed the *realness* so important to the credibility of the historical truth claims of the Bible. Biblical characters act in a way we might expect real people to react to real events in real time, not like fairy tales and myths. Once we get away from the inherent bias of most secular critics, the stories we read in our Bibles are compellingly real. We freely admit nobody comes to the biblical text free of presuppositions, including Christians. There is no perspectival neutrality about anything, least of all about a book claiming to be the ultimate window on the true nature of reality. Most secularists who still drink deeply of Enlightenment illusions are convinced they come to the Bible objectively; they don't because like any of us, they can't. We, on the other hand, who are open to the revelation of God in creation, can be open to the revelation of God in Scripture, which reveals to us the ultimate revelation of God in Christ.

END NOTES

INTRODUCTION
1. Timothy Keller, *The Reason for God: Belief in an Age of Skepticism* (London: Hodder & Stoughton, 2008), p. XVII.
2. C.S. Lewis, *Christian Reflections* (Grand Rapids, MI: Eerdmans, 1995), p. 164.

CHAPTER 1: THE BIBLE AND ITS CRITICS
1. The story of the intellectual history of the Enlightenment leading to the skepticism of David Hume, and eventually the hermeneutics of suspicion of much biblical criticism, is a long and complicated story filled with nuance and debate about cause and effect. Although the Enlightenment can come off as "the bad guy," and that is well deserved in many ways, not everything that came from it is bad. Many fruitful ideas have come from its thinkers and their ideas (some used in this book), but the underlying (unproven and unprovable) assumptions could not help but inevitably lead to the virulent anti-Christian secularism of our day.
2. Benjamin Wiker, *Moral Darwinism: How We Became Hedonists* (Downers Grove, IL: InterVarsity Press, 2002), p. 126.
3. I took the outline from a class I listened to online from Dr. Richard P. Belcher, Jr., of Reformed Theological Seminary on Genesis-Deuteronomy.
4. George Marsden, *The Soul of the American University: From Protestant Establishment to Established Nonbelief* (Oxford: Oxford University Press, 1994), P. 229.

5. N.T. Wright, *Jesus and the Victory of God* (Minneapolis: Fortress Press, 1996), p. 16, 17.
6. https://bible.org/article/survey-historical-jesus-studies-reimarus-wright#P38_11611. This is an excellent and concise overview by Michael H. Burer of what he calls historical Jesus studies.
7. The term higher criticism was initially used to distinguish it from "lower criticism," or textual criticism. This "lower" endeavor is a method used to determine what the original manuscripts of the Bible said, and most scholars, even the most skeptical, agree what we have written in our New Testament is pretty much what was written by the authors.
8. *The Fundamentals, Vol. 1*, Dyson Hague, "The History of Higher Criticism."
9. Leon Morris, *I Believe in Revelation* (Grand Rapids, MI: Eerdmans, 1976), p. 142.
10. Charles Hodge, *Systematic Theology, Vol. I* (Grand Rapids, MI: Eerdmans, 1982), p. 178.
11. Ibid., p. 65-66.
12. J. Gresham Machen, *Christianity & Liberalism*, (Grand Rapids, MI: Eerdmans Publishing Co., 1923).

CHAPTER 2: THE CHRISTIAN CONCEPT OF REVELATION
1. Benjamin B. Warfield, *The Inspiration and Authority of the Bible* (Phillipsburg, NJ: Presbyterian and Reformed Publishing, 1948), p. 72.
2. Herman Bavinck, *Our Reasonable Faith: A Survey of Christian Doctrine* (Grand Rapids, MI: Baker Book House, 1956), p. 35.
3. John Calvin, *Institutes of the Christian Religion 1* (Philadelphia, PA: The Westminster Press, 1960, Translated and Indexed by Ford Lewis Battles), p. 52.

4. I'm not arguing that God could not have used some kind of evolutionary processes or mechanisms in his creation of the world, only that it is either God or no God. When people use the term evolution today, they mean specifically Darwinian evolution, or random, unguided, material processes. By definition, Darwinism precludes God.
5. C.S. Lewis, *God in the Dock* (Grand Rapids, MI: Eerdmans, 1970), p. 15, 16.

CHAPTER 3: THE INSPIRATION AND AUTHORITY OF THE BIBLE

1. Loraine Boettner, *Studies in Theology* (Philadelphia, PA: Presbyterian and Reformed Publishing, 1965), p. 93.
2. Benjamin B. Warfield, *The Inspiration and Authority of the Bible* (Phillipsburg, NJ: Presbyterian and Reformed Publishing, 1948), p. 133.
3. John Murray, "The Attestation of Scripture," in *The Infallible Word: A Symposium* (Phillipsburg, NJ: Presbyterian and Reformed Publishing, 1948), p. 33.

CHAPTER 4: THE PEOPLE AND HISTORY OF ISRAEL

1. Thomas Cahill, *The Gifts of the Jews: How a Tribe of Desert Nomads Changed the Way Everyone Thinks and Feels* (New York: Anchor Books, 1998) p. 63.
2. Ibid., p. 95.

CHAPTER 5: JESUS — TOO POPULAR TO MAKE UP

1. C.S. Lewis, *Christian Reflections* (Grand Rapids, MI: Eerdmans, 1995), p. 155.
2. Martin Goodman, *Rome and Jerusalem: The Clash of Ancient Civilizations* (New York: Alfred A. Knopf, 2007), p. 59, 61.
3. Alfred Edersheim, *Sketches of Jewish Social Life* (Peabody, MA: Hendrickson, 1994), p. 64.

4. Ibid., p. 190.
5. Tom Holland, *Dominion: How the Christian Revolution Remade the World* (New York: Basic Books, 2019), p. 88.
6. Craig S. Keener, *The Historical Jesus of the Gospels* (Grand Rapids, MI: Cambridge, U.K.: Eerdmans, 2019), p. 330.
7. Richard Bauckham, *Jesus and the Eyewitnesses: The Gospels as Eyewitness Testimony* (Grand Rapids, MI: Eerdmans, 2017), p. 330.

CHAPTER 6: JESUS AND THE JEWISH NATURE OF HIS WORLD

1. Alfred Edersheim, *The Life and Times of Jesus the Messiah* (Peabody, MA: Hendrickson, 1993), p. 108.
2. F.F. Bruce, *The Spreading Flame* (Grand Rapids, MI: Eerdmans, 1958), p. 30.
3. Edersheim, Ibid., p. 64.
4. Martin Goodman, *Rome and Jerusalem: The Clash of Ancient Civilizations* (New York: Alfred A. Knopf, 2007), p. 192.
5. Geza Vermes, *Jesus the Jew: A Historian's Reading of the Gospels* (Philadelphia: Fortress Press, 1981), p. 131.
6. Edersheim, Ibid., p. 635.
7. Craig S. Keener, *The Historical Jesus of the Gospels* (Grand Rapids, MI: Eerdmans, 2009), p. 176.
8. Edersheim, Ibid., p. 102. Italics added.

CHAPTER 7: THE MIRACLES OF JESUS AND THE APOSTLES

1. R. Bultmann "New Testament and Mythology" in *Kerygma and Myth: A Theological Debate*. H.W. Bartsch (ed.), R.H. Fuller (trans.). (New York: Harper & Row, 1961), p.5.
2. C.S. Lewis, *Miracles: How God Intervenes in Nature and Human Affairs* (New York: Macmillan, 1978), p. 4.

3. Norman Geisler and Frank Turek, *I Don't Have Enough Faith to Be an Atheist* (Wheaton, IL: Crossway, 2004), p. 256 ff.
4. For the entire history of biblical criticism, scholars argued that the gospels, and Acts, were not eyewitness accounts, but kernels of historical events that were shaped over time by the needs of the Christian communities in which they grew, taking the shape we now have in our New Testament. This view, while still prevalent, is far from universal. Richard Bauckham's *Jesus and the Eyewitnesses: The Gospels as Eyewitness Testimony*, first published in 2006, has been an influential counter to the critical (skeptical) scholarly consensus.
5. Alfred Edersheim, *The Life and Times of Jesus the Messiah* (Peabody, MA: Hendrickson, 1993), p. 263.
6. F.F. Bruce, *The Spreading Flame* (Grand Rapids, MI: Eerdmans, 1958), p. 40.
7. Edersheim, Ibid., p. 471.

CHAPTER 8: JESUS' PERSONALITY — THE CONUNDRUM THAT WAS JESUS

1. Scottish minister John Duncan (1796-1870) seems to have first applied the term "trilemma" to this argument when he observed: "Christ either deceived mankind by conscious fraud, or he was himself deluded and self-deceived, or he was divine. There is no getting out of this trilemma. It is inexorable." It is often phrased, Jesus is either Lord, lunatic, or liar.
2. Alfred Edersheim, *The Life and Times of Jesus the Messiah* (Peabody, MA: Hendrickson, 1993), p. 542, 543.
3. Edersheim, Ibid., p. 710.
4. Timothy Keller, *Making Sense of God: An Invitation to the Skeptical* (New York: Viking, 2016), p. 228.
5. J.P. Moreland, *Scaling the Secular City: A Defense of Christianity* (Grand Rapids, MI: Baker Book House, 1987), p. 139.

6. Keller, Ibid., p. 242.
7. Tom Gilson, *Too Good to Be False: How Jesus' Incomparable Character Reveals his Reality* (Tampa, FL: DeWard, 2020), p. 154.

CHAPTER 9: JESUS' TEACHING
1. Alfred Edersheim, *The Life and Times of Jesus the Messiah* (Peabody, MA: Hendrickson, 1993), p. 368.
2. Edersheim, Ibid., p. 353.
3. John Ralson Saul, *Voltaire's Bastards: The Dictatorship of Reason in the West* (New York: The Free Press, 1992), p. 542.
4. Craig L. Blomberg, "Where Do We Start Studying Jesus," in *Jesus Under Fire: Modern Scholarship Reinvents the Historical Jesus* (Grand Rapids, MI: Zondervon, 1995), p. 33.
5. Geza Vermes, *Jesus the Jew: A Historian's Reading of the Gospels* (Philadelphia: Fortress Press, 1981), p. 224.
6. Timothy Keller, *The Reason for God: Belief in an Ages of Skepticism* (London: Hodder & Stoughton, 2008), p. 196.

CHAPTER 10: JESUS' BIRTH AND DEATH
1. Michael Green, "Jesus in the New Testament," in *The Truth of God Incarnate*, edited by Michael Green, 17-57. (London: Hodder & Stoughton, 1977.) Found in Peter S. Williams, *Getting at Jesus: A Comprehensive Critique of Neo-Atheist Nonsense About the Jesus of History* (Eugene, OR: Wipf & Stock, 2019), p. 112.
2. Geza Vermes, *Jesus the Jew: A Historian's Reading of the Gospels* (Philadelphia: Fortress Press, 1981), p. 215.
3. Alfred Edersheim, *The Life and Times of Jesus the Messiah* (Peabody, MA: Hendrickson, 1993), p. 102, 131.
4. Vermes, Ibid., p. 52 & 54.
5. Daniel Darling, *The Characters of Christmas: The Unlikely People Caught Up in the Story of Jesus* (Chicago: Moody Publishers, 2019), p. 50.

6. Martin Hengel, *Crucifixion* (Philadelphia: Fortress Press, 1977), p. 37, 38, 5, 10.
7. Ibid., p. 15.
8. Tom Holland, *Dominion: How the Christian Revolution Remade the World* (New York: Basic Books, 2019), p. 7.
9. Vermes, Ibid., p. 58.
10. Alfred Edersheim, *Sketches of Jewish Social Life* (Peabody, MA, Hendrickson, 1994), p. 267.
11. J. Gresham Machen, *The Origin of Paul's Religion* (Kindle edition), location 1017.
12. Peter S. Williams, Ibid., p. 110.
13. John Calvin, *Commentaries on the Epistle to the Hebrews* (Baker Book House, Grand Rapids: 1984), p. 36.

CHAPTER 11: THE RESURRECTION

1. C.S. Lewis, *God in the Dock: Essays on Theology and Ethics* (Grand Rapids, MI: Eerdmans), p. 102.
2. J. Gresham Machen, *The Origin of Paul's Religion* (Kindle edition), location 3604.
3. William Lane Craig, "Did Jesus Raise from the Dead," in *Jesus Under Fire: Modern Scholarship Reinvents the Historical Jesus* (Grand Rapids: Zondervon, 1995), p. 150.
4. Craig, Ibid., p. 148.
5. Timothy Keller, *The Reason for God: Belief in an Age of Skepticism* (London: Hodder & Stoughton, 2008), p. 202.
6. Quoted in Peter S. Williams, *Getting at Jesus: A Comprehensive Critique of Neo-Atheist Nonsense About the Jesus of History* (Eugene, OR: Wipf & Stock, 2019), p. 318.
7. Norman Geisler and Frank Turek, *I Don't Have Enough Faith to Be an Atheist* (Wheaton, IL: Crossway, 2004), p. 287.
8. Craig S. Keener, *The Historical Jesus of the Gospels* (Grand Rapids, MI: Eerdmans, 2009), p. 331.

9. In Nancy Pearcey's book *Saving Leonardo*, she describes the scene of Peter's denial as "completely unique" because "the Bible broke down the classical rules of style." There was no "antique genre" like it, which adds to the improbability that it could be a mere human invention (p. 154).
10. J.P. Moreland, *Scaling the Secular City: A Defense of Christianity* (Grand Rapids: Baker Book House, 1987), p. 179.
11. Moreland, Ibid., P. 180.

CHAPTER 12: THE APOSTLE PAUL
1. Martin Goodman, *Rome and Jerusalem: The Clash of Ancient Civilizations* (New York: Alfred A. Knopf, 2007), p. 493.
2. J. Gresham Machen, *The Origin of Paul's Religion* (Kindle edition), location 432.
3. Machen, Ibid., Location 109.
4. Machen, Ibid., Location 2600.
5. Machen, Ibid., Location 3034.
6. Alfred Edersheim, *Sketches of Jewish Social Life* (Peabody, MA: Hendrickson, 1994), p. 36.
7. Machen, Ibid., Location 1013.
8. Machen, Ibid., Location 3199.
9. Tom Holland, Dominion: *How the Christian Revolution Remade the World* (New York: Basic Books, 2019), p. 87.

CONCLUDING THOUGHTS
1. George Marsden's *The Soul of the American University: From Protestant Establishment to Established Nonbelief* is an excellent overview of the inexorable move over the last 200 years in higher education from orthodox Christianity to the intolerant secularism of today.

ACKNOWLEDGEMENTS

I would like to thank my wife, Sarah, for giving me the space to spend an inordinate amount of time in my office on my avocation of writing. She would testify that it's an obsession, and she would be right. Along with my daughter Gabrielle, and son Dominic, they read the manuscript and offered valuable suggestions I trust helped me improve the end product. I would also like to thank those who have come before, living and not, who have grappled with, studied, and written about the issues in this book. I am, as is said, a midget standing on the shoulders of giants who came before.

I would also like to give a shoutout to Tom Gilson whose feedback before the book went to the final edit, thankfully, was invaluable, and made this in my estimation a much better book.

Lastly, I would like to thank the team at Two Penny Publishing. Having published my first book by myself (quite an ordeal), it was a blessing having a team of professionals on which to rely. I had knowledgeable guides each step of the way who directed me through my ignorance to publish a book I trust is worthy of all the effort.

Soli Deo Gloria.

ABOUT THE AUTHOR

Mike D'Virgilio has a B.S. in Communication from Arizona State University and an M.A. in Systematic Theology from Westminster Theological Seminary Philadelphia. He has worked in public relations, sales, and marketing for over three decades. His first book was an exploration of apologetics for parents called, *The Persuasive Christian Parent: Building an Enduring Faith in You and Your Children*. He also wrote a love letter in the form of a short book to his wife and children called, *Our Story: Mike & Sarah D'Virgilio's Excellent Adventure (Courtship)*. He has also written for a variety of blogs over the years and is currently working his way through the Bible posting his thoughts at **mikedvirgilio.wordpress.com**. He also blogs on apologetics and a variety of topics at **mikedvirgilio.com**.

Made in United States
North Haven, CT
02 June 2023

37203023R00104